Cooking the Middle Eastern Way

Eat together and do not eat separately,
for the blessing is with the company.
Hadith, or saying of the Prophet Muhammad.

Foreword

As you might imagine, I had many adventures in my endeavours to learn the secrets of Middle Eastern cooking.

Most unusual was a lunch in North Yemen in a restaurant no bigger than a large hole in the wall. This is precisely what it was, a cavity in the wall around the capital, Sana'a, into which an enterprising Yemeni had manoeuvred some tables and chairs.

I had not finished eating when the space was invaded by crowds of men who, unable to squeeze past, walked across the top of my table. Then, finding a seat, they unclipped daggers and hung them on a hook as a Westerner might his umbrella. No one paid me, the only woman, the slightest attention. As far as they knew, I might have been a *djinn!*

Quite the opposite was a lavish banquet in Saudi Arabia in honour of the visit by Her Majesty Queen Elizabeth and the Duke of Edinburgh.

All that day refrigerated vans had sped the best of Arab and imported delicacies between Riyadh, the Saudi capital, and a spot in the desert, marked by a mammoth tent. Lobster had been flown in from Jeddah, and truffles from France, and fifty lambs had been slaughtered for the occasion, which was to be attended by hundreds of sheikhs. The hospitable Saudis had even extended the invitation to include the press – an unheard-of event in royal circles – which was how I found myself dining with the Queen, Her Majesty being obscured, however, by pyramids of dates.

Between these two remarkable occasions lie a wealth of memories and a host of meals – of which many are recaptured in *Cooking the Middle Eastern Way*.

The current interest in Middle Eastern cooking is part of a Western trend towards ethnic food. It also coincides with two significant events which, sadly, typify the Middle East in Western minds.

The first is the agonizing civil war in Lebanon which has uprooted many thousands of Lebanese who have fled abroad and taken their cuisine with them. Many have subsequently opened restaurants so that today one can eat Middle Eastern food in almost any large city in the world.

The second event, more protracted, has been the nationalization of the Arab oil industry. Inestimable wealth disbursed by generous rulers now enables even the poorest Bedouin to enjoy a vacation abroad. The first tourists brought cooks to prepare meals according to Muslim dietary laws, and it was not long before leading hotels in London and Paris were employing Muslim chefs, exposing Westerners to Middle Eastern cuisine.

The taste for Middle Eastern food was brought to Britain by business travellers and tour groups returning from trips. Expatriates employed in places such as Iraq and Iran also enthused about ethnic cooking.

In consequence there is an enormous curiosity about Middle Eastern cooking, but most restaurants serve only a limited number of dishes. This does not mean that *Cooking the Middle Eastern Way* will unveil a thousand and one recipes; what it will do is pass on a few of the most popular so that anyone with a moderate knowledge of cooking can make them.

Other recipes are missing for obvious reasons. It is not feasible to try smoking Iraqi *mashgouf* around a fire in your kitchen. Nor to cook *khouzi*, an Arab recipe requiring a whole sheep. Without help, sweetmeats such as *knaffeh* and Turkish Delight are very time-consuming to prepare. Today's Middle Eastern housewife usually buys them ready-made.

Bread is also frequently purchased from the baker who makes several batches throughout the day. Many breads are too big to bake in a domestic oven and are cooked in a large, beehive-shaped oven or *tanour*. Similar

types are sold in Lebanese and Turkish food shops or failing this, the Greek *pita* and Indian *naan* are similar. On a recent visit to Sydney I discovered *khoubz* in a supermarket.

An Australian, I was brought up on beef, but since leaving Sydney in 1963, I have travelled extensively in the Muslim world. By now I have visited every country in the Middle East – and North Africa for good measure.

My interest in local food developed after an initial visit to Beirut, the focus of Middle Eastern cookery. Like any Western visitor, I was eager to acquire some recipes in order to entertain at home. I did not want anything too elaborate, since like most working women, cooking time is limited to weekends, but I sought some easily prepared dishes for entertaining on busy week nights.

I trust the same applies to you and that *Cooking the Middle Eastern Way* will bring new pleasures to your table. *Bismillah!*★

CHRISTINE OSBORNE, 1985

★*Bismillah!* (in the name of God!), as expressed by an Arab before eating.

Left   *Pounding coffee beans with a traditional wooden mihbash, Jordan.*

Introduction

edia coverage of the sad events in Lebanon, or the Gulf War, gives the impression that the Middle East is a land of blazing guns, yet the millions of citizens going to work in Cairo or Ankara, or the *felaheen* toiling in the fields, represent a far more accurate picture of daily life.

The belly of the Orient, the Middle East sweeps east from Egypt through the countries of the Fertile Crescent as far as Iran and encompasses the vast land mass of the Arabian peninsula. The majority of people speak Arabic and share a common heritage with colourful regional variations in music, costume and cuisine.

While parts of the Middle East are largely desert, elsewhere is as green as the Cotswolds, as the name, the Fertile Crescent, implies. Other areas are even subtropical like the beautiful palm-fringed coast of Dhofar, in southern Oman, but between these extremes is the rugged Middle East of Bedouin nomads, a mix of pebble plain and dunes.

According to archaeologists and historians, civilization began sometime in the fifth millennium BC in Mesopotamia.

We know little about the diet of the ancient peoples but it seems likely that they had the same pulse-based diet as the *felaheen* of today, and because the region was rich in game, grilled gazelle and wild boar were probably popular.

Ancient civilizations and conquering armies have bequeathed to the Middle East a rich architectural heritage: the remains of giant dams, soaring pyramids, and magical-sounding cities such as Persepolis, Petra and Jerash. In the absence of records, one can only assume that peoples of such building expertise also possessed sophisticated culinary skills.

The expansion of the Greek and Roman empires undoubtedly contributed to the cuisine in the Middle East, and the spread of Islam from Arabia introduced humble but wholesome foods.

Ruling from Baghdad, the Abbasid dynasty (AD 786–902) is known to have been passionately interested in cooking. Many popular present-day recipes have origins in Abbasid kitchens.

The Ottoman Empire, introduced the stuffed vegetable dishes so popular in Middle Eastern cookery. British and French mandates following the First World War also added new ideas, but by now Middle Eastern cooking styles were firmly established and while Western dishes were applauded, local habits remained unchanged.

The amalgam of so many cuisines makes Middle Eastern food different and at the same time hard to define. Basically it can be described as wholesome and well-flavoured, spicy without being fiery-hot, and notable for several items in particular: *mezze* or starters, stuffed vegetables and meats and rich sweetmeats. It is not merely the food, however, which ranks Middle Eastern cooking – not before time – with the world's greatest cuisines, but its presentation and the surroundings in which it is served.

REGIONAL COOKING
THE LEVANT

While Middle Eastern cooking follows a basic theme, there are regional variations: Levantines eat more grilled meat and yoghurt than, say, the Yemenis; Yemenis, on the other hand, like spicy dishes; Persian recipes dabble in a subtle combination of fruit and meat; curries have crept into the Arab cuisine, etc. There is little difference in etiquette except where contact with the West has influenced customs.

The countries of the eastern Mediterranean littoral, or the Levant – Lebanon, Syria and Jordan – enjoy a similar cuisine; however the same dish may be called by different names, which is rather confusing, in the same way that cooking methods – a pinch of this, or a handful of that – are often vague. Of the three cuisines, Jordanian

Opposite above left *A fine bream in Muscat. The Omanis are great fish-eaters.*

Opposite above right *Sifting pulses in Aswan, Upper Egypt.*

Opposite below left *A Bedouin woman making buttermilk in Dubai.*

Opposite below right *Tomato-seller in an East Jerusalem souq or bazaar.*

cooking is more basic, a mix of Bedouin food from the eastern desert and warming dishes from the Western escarpment. Syrian cooking tends to be more elaborate, while the best known, Lebanese, is noted for the stylish presentation of food and the infinite variety of dishes.

The flavours of Lebanon are those most commonly associated with Middle Eastern cookery: the tangy taste of chopped mint, garlic and lemon juice in an olive oil dressing; the smoky taste of purées made from roasted sesame seeds and grilled aubergines; the subtle taste of rose water in desserts. While the aroma of Turkish coffee percolates the entire Middle East, this too, is unmistakably Lebanese.

If any race lives to eat, it is the affable Lebanese; a nation of shrewd businessmen who find any excuse a good reason to mix business with the pleasure of eating.

The Arabic, *lebnan*, is derived from an Aramaic word meaning white, a reference to the snow-covered mountains behind Beirut but also to *laban* which in Lebanon, means curdled milk, a dish of thick, creamy yoghurt being a popular *mezze*.

Mezze or starters are the best known aspect of Lebanese cuisine. They consist of many small dishes, either true *hors d'oeuvre* or miniature main courses, laid out for people to serve themselves as in a Scandinavian *smörgasbord*. Some of the endless *mezze* recipes are described in the first chapter.

A typical meal may consist solely of *mezze* or have several courses such as stuffed meat and vegetable dishes, *kebabs*, a fish or poultry dish, salads and rice, ending with fresh fruit, sweetmeats and coffee. A water pipe, or *nargila*, may be brought in for the men, its gentle bubbling adding to the convivial atmosphere.

Arak is commonly drunk with a *mezze*. Lebanon also produces wines. The Lebanese particularly like eating out of doors, it being debatable whether they, or the Turks, invented the custom of *al fresco* dining.

Syrian food lacks the variety of Lebanese, but it is invariably appetizing. *Mezze* are equally a Syrian tradition. *Bulghur* is widely used in

Right   *Elaborate silver tamarind juice stand in Damascus, Syria.*

Far right   *A rural baker in Iran. The large loaves of barbari are too big for a domestic oven.*

cooking and Syrian housewives are reputedly the best *kibbeh* makers in the Middle East. Seafood is available on the Mediterranean coast.

Part of the Fertile Crescent, Syria is self-sufficient in vegetables and fruits – pears, grapes and delicious figs. Preserved apricots are a speciality of Damascus. Together with almonds and walnuts, pistachio nuts are used in the sweetmeats at which Syrian pastrycooks excel. Aleppo is renowned for superb pastries and rich desserts.

Syria produces similar fruity wines to the Lebanon. *Arak* is drunk with *mezze*. Traditional fruit juices— tamarind, orange and pomegranate – are losing ground to bottled soft drinks. Tea is drunk at every opportunity. Coffee is always served with a large glass of water to quench the thirst. Yoghurt-and-water is drunk by the Bedouin.

Several Jordanian dishes have roots in Bedouin cooking.

The best example is *mansaf,* meaning "the large tray" or dish on which this traditional repast is served. A vast communal dinner, it consists of slices of stewed mutton, rice, bread and *jameed* (a dried sheep's milk yoghurt crumbled, melted and poured over the food). Similar to the Arab *khouzi, mansaf* is served on the floor of a tent with everyone sitting around the dish helping himself.

Fatir is a popular people's food, consisting of unleavened bread soaked in yoghurt and topped with *samneh* (or clarified butter).

In Amman *mezze* are popular: variations are *kishki,* or yoghurt mixed with chopped walnuts and olive oil and sprinkled with the lemony spice known as *sumak*. Most *mezze* are an extension of Lebanese cuisine.

Soups are not widespread, perhaps because of the rich sauces which accompany many main courses. Soups made from lentils, meat and vegetables and *frieka* (cracked smoked wheat) are most common, especially in the Western

escarpment overlooking the Dead Sea.

Popular main courses are: *yakneh* (a meat and vegetable casserole), *mahshi* or stuffed vegetables, chicken and *kebabs*. *Shawarma* (sliced lamb on a skewer) is equally popular in Jordan as it is in Syria or Lebanon.

Like poultry, meat is marinated to tenderise and to absorb flavours. A common custom adds coriander fried with garlic to many recipes: a small wooden pestle and mortar used solely for grinding this mixture is kept in every kitchen. Common vegetables in Jordanian cooking are tomatoes, okra, cabbage and aubergines. Rice is more popular as a side dish there than in Syria or Lebanon, a custom linked to basic Bedouin cooking.

Shops in Amman specialize in *knaffeh,* a cream cheese sweetmeat with Palestinian origins. Most local sweetmeats are made throughout the Levant.

Bread is eaten with every meal with many variations on the common, rounded unleavened pocket bread known simply as *khoubz*. People buy *ka'ik bil sim-sim,* a soft bread ring sprinkled with sesame seeds, sold with a boiled egg and a tiny packet of spices, to eat on their way to work.

TURKEY

Ottoman domination of the Middle East had a big influence on ethnic cooking. Many recipes have Turkish origins: who but the Turks would call dishes "Dainty Fingers" or "Lady's Thighs"– *kadın budu?*

The Ottoman sultans' opulent tastes also extended to the kitchen. The largest parts of the Topkapi Palace were the kitchens where we are told that some sixty chefs and two hundred assistants devised special delicacies. It is said they had at least forty ways of cooking aubergine and more than sixty ways of making *baklava*. There were specialists for *böreks* (stuffed pastries), cooks for fish, meat and poultry, and makers of sweetmeats.

Based on meat and dairy products,

The subtle use of herbs and spices is a feature of Middle Eastern recipes. Many are native to the region.

Turkish food is high in protein. Plain yoghurt is greatly enjoyed, blended into soups and sauces, or as a flavour in cakes. White cheese is always found in a *meze* (*mezze*) with other starters.

Seafood is popular on the coast while lamb is the basic meat, the *döner kebap* (turning kebab) has travelled to the far corners of the earth with Turkish migrants. *Döner kebap* (*shawarma* in Arabic) slowly turning on a skewer is a familiar sight. Pieces of lamb are loaded onto a vertical skewer which slowly turns in front of an electric grill. As they cook, they are sliced off into a tray or, if a customer is waiting, into a pocket of *ekmek* (*pita* bread) which is filled with salad.

Turkish cooks perform miracles with the most mundane vegetables. Plain by most standards, the cabbage is elevated to regal status by stuffing with rice, raisins and pine nuts. The stuffed aubergine dish *Imam bayıldı* (swooning Imam) has captured the imagination of cooks far beyond the Middle East.

Rice is habitually served with main courses; Turks like long-grain rice cooked so that a little moisture remains.

Desserts are those based on milk, such as *muhallabia*, or rice pudding, and those made from pastry such as *baklava*. The most famous sweetmeat is *lokum*, known all over the world as Turkish

Delight.

Traditional beverages are beer, wine and *rakı* (arak). Made from grapes and aniseed, *rakı* clouds when water is added giving it the popular name of *Aslan sutu* or "lion's milk." Other drinks are *aryan* (yoghurt and water) and *shira* or grape juice. Turkish coffee is served *şekersiz* (without sugar), *orta şekerli* (medium) or *şerkerli* (plenty of sugar).

EGYPT
The origins of some Egyptian recipes can be traced back to the Pharaonic times. It is fascinating to consider that *bamieh* or okra stew and *melokhia* leaf soup were as popular then as they are today but it is a disappointment not to find a grand dish that epitomises Egyptian cooking.

Most recipes contain elements from the whole range of foods generally thought of as Middle Eastern fare, while the *cous-cous* of North Africa is popular. Occupying armies have also influenced the local repertoire and whether the famous *Umm Ali* pudding is actually British or Egyptian is something of a moot question.

The peasant dish *foul medames* (brown bean casserole) is eaten by three-quarters of the population before work.

While most middle class Egyptian households serve *mezze*, they do not reach the elaborate proportions of the Levant. Eaten dipped in *tahini*, *falafel* (butter bean rissoles) are a great favourite.

Poultry is greatly prized. Otherwise famous for nightclubs, Kasr el Nil, the avenue leading to the Pyramids, is equally famous for restaurants specializing in roast pigeon.

The Nile Valley produces wonderful vegetables. Citrus fruits are plentiful, the round green lime having a special place in local cooking. Fruit juices – grape, orange and lemon, tamarind and mango – are popular. Tea is widely drunk.

Popular desserts are *Umm Ali* and *muhallabia*, while an old family cook who used to work for the British is sure to produce a good pudding. *Baklava* and *basbousa* are among many sweetmeats. Groppi's tea-room in Cairo is a popular rendezvous for tea and pastries.

ARAB STATES
Apart from Yemen, the cooking is similar throughout Arabia (Saudi Arabia, Bahrain, Kuwait, Qatar, the United Arab Emirates and the Sultanate of Oman). Prior to the wealth from oil and gas deposits, the Arabs lived on a Bedouin diet of dates, rice, and meat when it was available. The coastal communities also ate fish.

All the Arab states enjoy splendid seafood. While the *souqs* and supermarkets are stocked with everything money can buy, some countries have become self-sufficient in certain foods, thus increasing the scope for cooking. The Emirate of Ras al-Khaimah produces milk from cattle living in air-conditioned stalls, while Abu Dhabi grows excellent vegetables.

The large number of Indians and Bangladeshis employed as cooks has resulted in many dishes becoming hotter and spicier. On the coast, people are exposed to new foods in hotels. *Mezze* have become an accepted start to a meal and a Kuwaiti, or a Bahraini, enjoys spaghetti just as much as an Italian.

The Arabs eat only *basmati* rice. Dried Indian or Omani limes are ground into a powder which, added to food, imparts an unusual tart flavour.

Popular main courses are braised meat with potatoes, *kebabs*, fish and prawn or chicken curries. *Khouzi* is a famous Arab dish prepared on auspicious occasions such as a tribal wedding, or the inauguration of a new airport. In former times, the recipe called for a whole baby camel to be stuffed with a whole sheep stuffed with whole chickens in turn stuffed with hard-boiled eggs and the rest of the cavity stuffed with rice, nuts, raisins and spices. Today a sheep is similarly stuffed and cooked for several hours in a huge *tanour*. When the flesh is tender the carcass is removed and the stuffing spread on top for people to serve themselves.

Such a feast is served on the floor of the living room, or tent. VIPs sit on either side of the host, who breaks off tasty pieces and passes them around. Contrary to the rather morbid Western preoccupation with the Arab taste for sheep's eyes, the brains and spleen are considered the choice morsels.

Mineral water, soft drinks or yoghurt drinks are common beverages.

Fruit and dates are served after dinner. Oases near Nizwa, in the rugged interior of Oman, produce some of the best dates in Arabia. *Muhammar*, a sweetened rice, is popular.

Coffee, usually Nescafé, and sweet black tea are served afterwards. *Qahwa*, coffee brewed with cardamom husks, is offered ritually on other occasions.

YEMEN

Traditional Yemeni food is unknown outside Yemen, a wildly beautiful country barely out of the Middle Ages.

Local diet is based on several highly original dishes that can be attributed to the country's long isolation. Others show an Ottoman influence, while a taste for spicy foods results from contact with Indian traders on the Tihama or Red Sea coast.

Food is always fresh. No Yemeni housewife would dream of dishing up leftovers; what is not eaten is distributed among the less fortunate. A negative side is that most dishes are served boiling hot and thus lose their nutritional value. Due to economic restraints, few dishes are very nourishing and the truly unique Yemeni recipes are unlikely to appeal to a Western palate. Others common to Middle Eastern cookery – lentil soup, okra stew – appear in this book.

Bread is the basis of every meal; the most common is a round, unleavened bread baked from sorghum flour, which is ground by the housewife or taken to the local miller. *Bint al sahin* is a cross between bread and a pudding, eaten hot as a savoury dish or smothered with *samneh* and honey.

The consumption of fresh milk is rare. Sheep or goat's milk is soured by prolonged vigorous shaking in a gourd, the resultant buttermilk being used in the preparation of many dishes. Farmers in the Tihama foothills make a first class smoked goat's milk cheese, known as *jubn*, which is sold in Ta'iz, the old capital.

Soups are popular, especially in the cooler highlands. The most common is *helba*, based on ground fenugreek seeds which are whipped to a froth, with meat stock, hot pepper and other seasonings.

Similar to the Levant, dips are a tradition, but in Yemen they are different. *Zahawiq*, the best known, is made from tomatoes and chilli to which tiny dried fish are sometimes added. *Foul* is eaten daily. Other pulses are made into stews. *Asid* is a thick gruel-like porridge made from sorghum, boiling water, oil and honey or broth. Mutton is the most common meat, the brain and liver being especially revered.

Most days Yemenis forego breakfast in favour of a large lunch before the *qat*-chewing session. Chewed every afternoon, the leaf depresses the appetite, supper in consequence being late and light. On market day, breakfast is a tradition for farmers who travel long distances. Typical breakfasts are chick peas served with fried liver, *fattah* (a dough made from dates, bananas and butter) and *mattit* (egg, tomatoes, peppers and onions made into a soup mixed with crumbled bread, butter and honey).

Most foods are cooked in vegetable oils. *Alya*, lard obtained from the melted down fatty tail of sheep, is popular in rural areas. Cooking

facilities remain primitive; most women cook over a fire in the kitchen, or at the entrance to their house. When something special is made, it is a custom to send a portion to a neighbour.

When the meal is ready, everyone sits around the cloth, unless strangers are present, when women eat separately. Traditionally served first, men receive the choicest portions of food (a custom throughout the entire Middle East).

A meal is eaten in a special order. The first course is white radish, which is dipped in *helba*. A salad follows, with *bint al sahin*, soup and hot vegetable dishes such as okra and potatoes. The last course is usually mutton stew, or grilled chicken with rice. This menu is typical of a middle class urban family; most Yemenis eat a lot less.

Special foods are eaten during the fast of Ramadan. Similar to other countries in the Middle East, the fast is broken with dates, grapes and other fruits, followed by a large meal. In the mountains, soups replace gruel, while *muhallabia* is a popular Ramadan dessert.

IRAN

Persian cooking is very sophisticated, a fact not generally known outside Iran. While the country has an advantage over the Arab states in being largely agricultural, local recipes display real genius in combining many unusual ingredients. A good example is meat and prune casserole. Dried fruit soups are also typically Persian.

Bread is served with every meal, an eating aid rather than a food to enjoy.

Salads and starters are essential components of a meal. Lettuce and tomato salad and cucumber salad with raisins and yoghurt are very popular.

Thick yoghurt is the base of many salads or *borani* served as starters, or *pish ghaza*. Similar to *mezze*, these may consist of as many as forty small dishes and soups set out as a buffet.

An elaborate table setting during Eid al-fitr, the holiday following Ramadan, the month of fasting.

Main courses cover a variety of mutton and chicken dishes, usually roasted or stewed with the addition of herbs and spices. Cooked slowly, the sauces become rich and aromatic; some become so thick that when poured over rice they make a substantial meal.

The most famous Persian dish is *chelo kebab*. The best cuts of lamb are thinly sliced and marinated in onion and lemon juice. After brief cooking over hot coals, they are arranged on a cushion of fluffy rice. Dabs of butter and a raw egg yolk are mixed into the rice and *sumak* is sprinkled on top. Slivers of onion, radishes and sprigs of parsley are served as garnishes. A queue outside a restaurant indicates they serve good *chelo kebab*.

The various ways of cooking rice in Iran have no equal in the Middle East; popular are steamed rice or *chelo* (see page 76) and *katteh*, a moulded rice served in wedges.

The Iranian caviar fishing industry is centred in Babolsar on the Caspian Sea. The grey-green beluga caviar from the elephant sturgeon is the best quality. Sturgeon themselves are a great delicacy. The thick fillets are lightly smoked and served poached with a green lemon juice dressing. Rural restaurants serve grilled trout, while the Gulf cities enjoy good seafood in common with most Arab countries.

Desserts tend to be either rather heavy or very sweet, a general trend throughout the Middle East. Stuffed apples and quinces are very popular.

The country produces an abundance of fruits – oranges, peaches, pomegranates and succulent watermelons from the Isfahan Oasis. Many fruits are made into *sharbats* – from which the word *sorbet* derives.

Extolled by Farsi poets, Persian wine was of considerable quality, one of the main wine growing regions being around Shiraz, "the city of wine and roses." *Abdug* or yoghurt-and-water is drunk during a meal. People

drink tea rather than coffee.

IRAQ

The art of Middle Eastern cookery reached its zenith during the Abbasid era in Baghdad – the city of Sheherezade and "a thousand and one nights."

The culinary skills of Abbasid chefs were renowned: great chefs were presented at court, the lavishness of their creations was extolled by poets, and lengthy treatises were written on the noble art of cookery. Ancient cookery manuals refer to banquets lasting for days, with table after table laden with roast partridges, ducks and francolins that had been marinated overnight in curd; milk-fed kid and spitted gazelle, and platters of sweetmeats.

With the exception of one or two regional dishes, Iraqi cooking follows general trends with an historic Persian bias. While most Iraqis eat sparingly, when they do eat, it resembles a last supper. An Iraqi dining table is invariably loaded with exotic foods.

Starters are usually stuffed potatoes, *dolmas* and salads. Spiked with mint, yoghurt is popular, while rice dishes are similar to Persian varieties. The most elaborate, *timman za'fran*, includes minced meat, raisins and nuts – a substantial meal.

A variation on the famous Saudi *khouzi*, steams a whole lamb on a domestic stove, then barbecues it over a bed of rice in a *tanour*. Suspended head down, the fatty tail constantly bastes the carcass as it melts.

Parks and gardens line the Tigris River flowing through Baghdad, where restaurants are set out under the trees. A traditional dish is *mashgouf*, a delicious fish which is slowly smoked around an open fire and served with sliced tomatoes, onions and bread.

Fish and dates are twin products in Basra, at the head of the Arabian Gulf. Dates have a myriad uses – barbecued fish with date purée is typical of Basra,

Among themselves, most Arab families eat off a cloth spread on the living room floor. However, if a Western guest is present, a table will be set with crockery and cutlery.

dates are made into *halwa*, a toffee-like sweet, and stuffed in pastries.

Mentioned in the *Arabian Nights*, the sweet, orange-coloured rosettes known as *zlabiya* are still popular.

Sweetmeats and coffee are served in the living room. If people have used their fingers to eat, a servant may bring a jug of water and soap to wash. Most urban houses have Western-type bathrooms.

ETIQUETTE, CUSTOMS AND COOKING TIPS

Living an isolated existence in the desert, a Bedouin nomad displays the same characteristics as an American family out in the Midwest, or Australians in the outback. Hospitality is second nature: while having no idea from where their next meal may come, they will offer what they have – their last bread or dates. In extending their hospitality, reflected in the coffee ceremony (see pages 142 to 151), they consider it their duty to protect a guest, even a perfect stranger. As more and more Bedouin exchange nomadism for a sedentary life, these same unwritten rules apply in the city.

There are certain rules of etiquette in the Middle East which *Orientales*, as people refer to themselves, have observed since the revelations of the holy *Quran*. "Cleanliness is next to godliness", is a saying that may have come from Muslim society. It is unthinkable not to wash before saying one's prayers, or sitting down to eat. Even basic Arab restaurants have a corner basin. Incense is frequently burned to purify the air.

A strict code of etiquette at mealtimes expresses subtle distinctions among the diners. An important guest will be offered special delicacies such as the tail of the chicken, and so on. The host has the first taste, a custom to show the food is worthy of being eaten and to encourage others to eat.

A meal always commences with thanks to Allah, the provider – *bismillah!* Morsels of food are taken or accepted using only the right hand. One should never refuse pieces offered by one's host as it is considered impolite. If seated on the floor, the soles of one's feet must not be displayed as this, too, is considered ill-mannered. Other aspects of local etiquette are similar to Western table manners: not to fill one's mouth too full, not to finish eating first in order not to embarrass others.

DIETARY LAWS

Muslim dietary laws are prescribed in the *Quran*, the book of revelations of the Angel Gabriel to the Prophet Muhammed in sixth-century Arabia and later transcribed by his companions.

Food is frequently mentioned, the major rules being abstention from eating the flesh of swine, the blood of any animal, or indeed eating any animal that has not been slaughtered in the correct manner by a Muslim (*hilal*). Muslims slit the throat of a beast, at the same time repeating the phrase: "In the name of God, God is most great!" Alcoholic drinks are forbidden.

SPICES

Middle Eastern food is characterized by the subtle use of spices bought in the *attarine* or spice street, where traders squat in tiny shops among boxes of colourful spices.

While today the emphasis is on the value of spices as flavourings, they have always had uses as homeopathic remedies, as vegetable dyes and in purification rituals.

Cassia and cinnamon were essential components in Egyptian embalming oils. Frankincense and cinnamon were among the gifts taken by the Queen of Sheba on her historic journey to Jerusalem. Frankincense and myrrh were also offered to the infant Jesus in Bethlehem.

Contact with the East inevitably introduced spices to Western kitchens; crusading knights brought new ideas for flavourings; and the use of spices in

Abbasid society was second to none.

The following spices are commonly used in Middle Eastern cooking.

A native of the Middle East, anise is cultivated for its small, oil-bearing seeds. Allspice is a fragrant spice, like a blend of cinnamon, nutmeg and cloves. It is used in stuffings.

The Middle East is the world's biggest importer of cardamom, whose crushed seeds are blended with meat dishes, while the whole pods flavour desserts and coffee.

While paprika is used in many regions, hotter spices such as chilli powder are generally restricted to the Yemen. Cinnamon is used in a variety of dishes, while cloves are used to flavour veal and other dishes. Coriander is another native spice which Mesopotamian records claim was cultivated in the fabled hanging gardens of Babylon.

The "queen of spices", cumin, is also a native of the Middle East. Its delicate aroma complements many vegetable dishes and salads – *falafel* need a good pinch of cumin to enliven their flavour. Used ground, or whole, cumin is an ingredient in Gulf fish curries. Ground fenugreek seeds help thicken curries and are excellent served with potatoes and aubergines.

Ginger appears in many medieval recipes, its medicinal value being noted in the *Quran*. Ginger tea is a soothing beverage. Abbasid society used nutmeg as a remedy for intestinal disorders; today it is used as a flavour and decoration for desserts.

The world's most popular spice, pepper, is used to flavour savoury dishes, and if pepper tops the popularity poll, then saffron is the world's most expensive spice. It requires over 250,000 crocus stigmas to make a pound of saffron but only a few strands to give a beautiful glow to rice and poultry dishes. Turmeric, a yellow Indian spice, is a cheaper alternative, but no substitute in terms of flavour.

Sesame seed is an historically valuable spice in the Middle East. Raw or roasted, its seeds flavour many dishes and breads. The oil is used on salads and in cooking.

FESTIVALS

There are several important religious festivals in the Muslim calendar.

Eid al-fitr is observed on the tenth month, following Ramadan, the month of fasting, fasting from dawn until dusk being considered good self-discipline and spiritually uplifting.

It begins when the new moon is sighted over Mecca, in Saudi Arabia. Special sweets are made; *nahash*, a cream cheese and filo pastry, is a Syrian speciality made at this time.

COOKING UTENSILS

Being very old, most of the recipes in this book were originally cooked using unsophisticated utensils on primitive stoves. A modern person cooking the Middle Eastern way needs only three or four basic items in addition to normal kitchen utensils: a large, deep frying pan, preferably made of cast iron; a pestle and mortar; and a blender or food processor.

COOKING INGREDIENTS

Cooking oils are basically vegetable oils such as corn oil, sunflower oil or various nut oils. Dishes to be eaten cold are made with olive oil, which is the foundation of all dressings.

Samneh is melted butter, clarified by straining the oil through a thin piece of muslin which extracts any impurities and imparts a richer taste. Like *alya, samneh* is mainly used by rural communities.

Other items to have in stock for cooking the Middle Eastern way are *bulghur,* or cracked wheat; *tahina* or *tahini; filo* pastry; flavourings such as orange flower and rose water; and a supply of almonds, pine nuts, walnuts, and pistachios.

Mezze *(Hors d'oeuvre or Starters)*

Beirut used to be an enchanting city. Standing with its feet in the blue Mediterranean and with its back to snowcapped Mount Lebanon, it was cultured, sophisticated and fun-loving. It also had some of the finest restaurants in the Middle East.

I first visited Lebanon in 1970 to write some travel articles. Then in 1977 I returned to photograph war torn Beirut for *The Times*. It was a brief acquaintance, but one of special significance to my subsequent interest in Middle Eastern cookery.

On this initial visit, with a friend, we chose to eat in a restaurant at Pigeon Grotto, a popular family outing from Beirut. Having ordered *mezze*, we were choosing a main course when the *maître d'hôtel* suggested that *mezze* would probably suffice. Imagine our relief, therefore, when plate after plate of starters was brought to the table. Counted, they numbered twenty-five and were obviously a substantial meal.

Essentially a Lebanese creation, *mezze* assume the aura of a banquet when prepared by a cook of repute. A way of life in Lebanon, Syria and Turkey, *mezze* have been adopted by other countries in the Middle East. As many as seventy dishes may be served in a large *mezze* on an auspicious occasion such as a marriage.

Making a pocket-bread sandwich in a Cairo snackbar.

Next page   *Mezze or starters. A large mezze table may have up to 70 small dishes.*

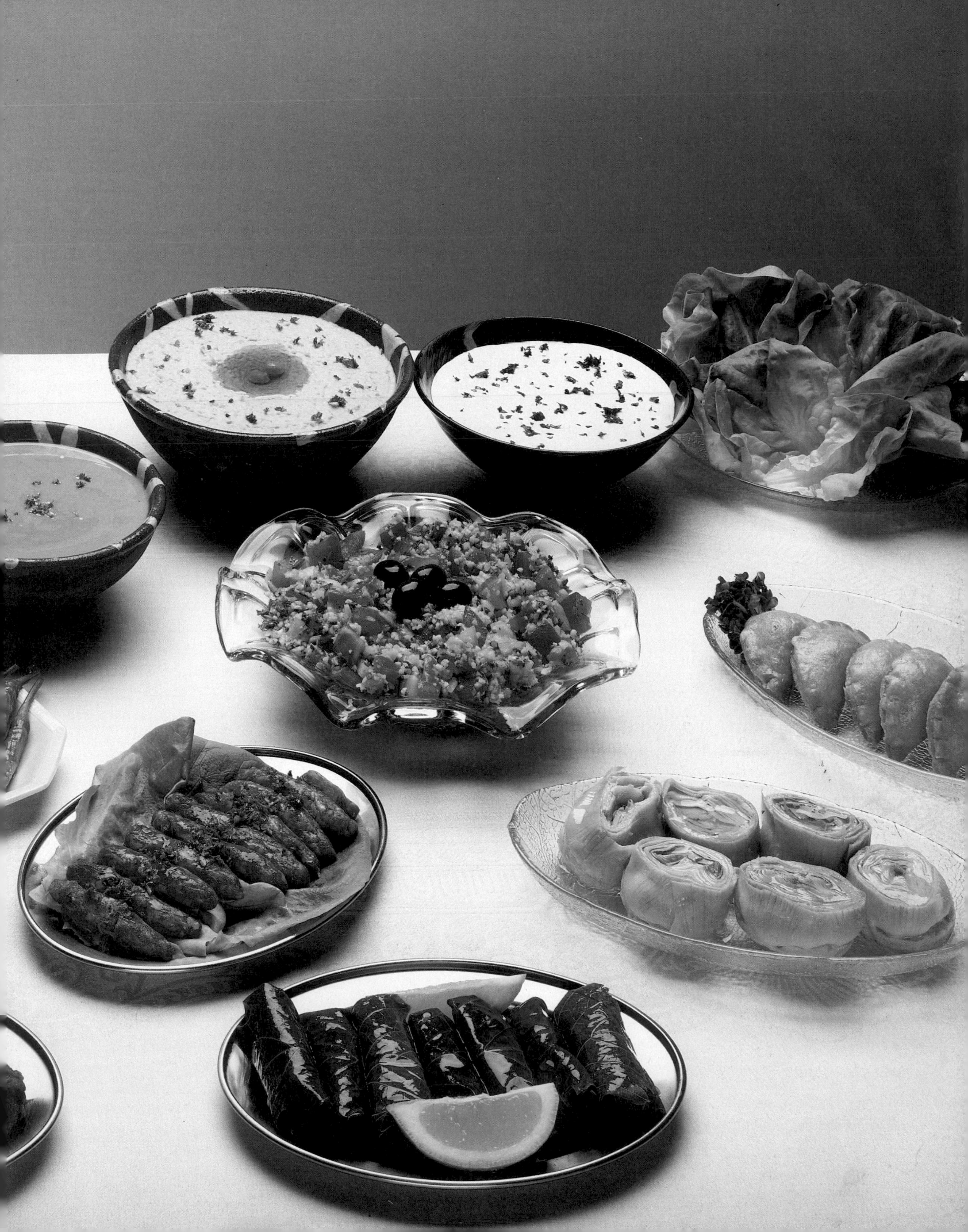

Items may be miniatures of a main course or true *hors d'oeuvre*, similar to a Scandinavian *smörgasbord*. Their preparation is time-consuming, but many *mezze* can be made beforehand and chilled. Others such as sautéed testicles should be served fresh for best results. Ideally you need someone to help, either to cook or to take the dishes to the table.

You can plan *mezze* around whatever you like, but there are about a dozen basic items without which even a small *mezze* is incomplete. First, the *mezze* table must always have a basket of freshly made bread; the round, unleavened bread known vaguely as *khoubz Arabieh*, which is used instead of cutlery to scoop up food. It is also essential for the dips.

Three or four dips are always found on a *mezze* table. The best known is *hummus*, a creamy, pale yellow dip made from mashed chick peas and *tahini* (a paste made from ground sesame seeds), blended with lemon juice and spices. Also popular is *babagannouj*, a pleasant, smoky-tasting dip made from grilled, mashed aubergine, garlic and *tahini*. I love it, one dish of *babagannouj* never being enough as I sit talking, dipping bread in it.

Taramasalata is flesh-coloured purée made from fish roe. Bread and celery sticks are dipped into *taramasalata* (which *must* be homemade). Made from strained yoghurt, thick, creamy *labneh* is always part of a *mezze*. In contrast, a purée of red pepper and walnuts, *muhammara*, is a hot dip. Both keep well in the refrigerator.

Another familiar constituent of *mezze* is stuffed vine leaves. These are popular throughout the Middle East,

either hot with a minced meat filling, or cold, stuffed with rice and pine nuts.

Lebanese cooking suffers from only one handicap in that there is no good beef available. This is true throughout the Middle East, which is not cattle country. As mutton is also frequently of poor quality, a great many seasonings are used to compensate for the lack of flavour, and meat is often minced to disguise the tough texture. Usually there are at least two minced meat dishes in a basic *mezze*. *Kibbeh nayé* consists of raw, seasoned minced lamb. This mixture can be combined with other ingredients, made into meatballs, and fried.

Strips of fried liver and *sanbusak* or *börek* (pastries) filled with minced meat, cream cheese and spinach, are also popular *mezze*. Artichoke hearts, brains (both with lemon and olive oil dressing), cubes of white cheese, celery, olives and pickled sweet peppers are easy-to-serve cold dishes. And one could go on endlessly listing more dishes – *falafel* (mashed butter bean or chick pea rissoles), fried mussels, chicken wings grilled with garlic and yoghurt sauce, miniature pizzas . . .

But, finally, there is *tabbouleh*, the Lebanese national salad, without which no *mezze* is complete. Very refreshing, it has a crunchy texture from the cracked wheat and a tangy taste from the lemon. It must be served fresh.

By tradition, *mezze* are eaten with *arak* (*raki* in Turkey), a spirit similar to *pastis* drinks such as Pernod.

Babagannouj *Aubergine Dip*

Serves about 4:
2 large aubergines
4 1/2 tablespoons
tahini (sesame seed paste)
juice of 2 lemons
2 cloves garlic, crushed
1/4 tablespoon salt
pepper, to taste
1 tablespoon finely chopped
parsley, to garnish
olive oil, to serve

Slit the skins of the aubergines – this will allow the steam to escape during cooking – then bake or grill gently until the outside is charred and crisp and it begins to split. Scoop out the pulp and mash thoroughly.

Combine with the *tahini*, lemon juice, garlic, salt and pepper and process or blend to a smooth consistency. If the mixture seems too thick, add some water – which will turn it a whiter colour.

Serve in a glass or pottery dish garnished with the chopped parsley and, finally, pour a teaspoon of olive oil into the centre.

Babagannouj is most often eaten as a dip with pita bread, but it can also be served as a salad with black olives and tomato slices.

Babagannouj is a smoky dip made from grilled aubergines.

Hummus *Chick Pea Dip*

Serves about 6:
175 g (6 oz) chick peas
1 teaspoon bicarbonate of soda
1-2 garlic cloves, crushed
salt
150 ml (5 fl oz) tahini paste
juice of 2-3 lemons
3 tablespoons olive oil
paprika, to sprinkle
finely chopped parsley, to garnish

Soak the chick peas in plenty of cold water overnight. Drain, add the bicarbonate of soda, cover with water and cook in a pressure-cooker for about 20 minutes, or simmer for 1½ hours in a pan. Drain the chick peas, reserving the liquid, then set aside a few peas for garnish.

Using a little of the cooking liquid, reduce the rest of the chick peas to a purée in a blender or processor. Add the garlic, salt and *tahini*, and blend together thoroughly. Lastly pour in the lemon juice, by which time the

hummus should have a rich, creamy consistency.

Pour into a shallow, concave dish (about the size of a salad plate), pour the oil in the centre and garnish with the whole chick peas. Sprinkle the paprika and a little chopped parsley as a decoration around the edges.

Hummus should be served at room temperature as a dip with warmed pita bread. It also makes a tasty accompaniment to grilled kebabs.

Taramasalata *Fish Roe Dip*

Serves about 4:
4 thick slices stale white bread
4 1/2 tablespoons cold milk
100 g (4 oz) fish roe (see method)
1 clove garlic, crushed
1/2 small onion, finely minced
juice of 1-2 lemons, to taste
1 egg yolk
4 1/2 tablespoons olive oil

The most authentic roe to use is *tarama*, the dried and salted roe of the grey mullet. Smoked cod's roe can be used instead, in which case the skins will need to be removed first.

Remove the crusts and soak the bread in the cold milk. Meanwhile, beat the roe thoroughly in a mortar or in a blender until it is soft.

Squeeze the bread dry and crumble into the roe. Add the garlic and onion, half the lemon juice and beat (or blend) to a creamy paste. When it is smooth, break in the egg yolk and

continue to beat or blend while dribbling in the olive oil and the rest of the lemon juice.

Chill and serve as a dip with whole radishes, black olives, celery sticks, and pita bread.

Most *taramasalata* sold commercially is artificially coloured and tastes nothing like this. The home-made version will keep for about 10 days in a sealed container in the refrigerator.

Tahini *Sesame Paste Dip*

Serves about 4:
2 cloves garlic
salt, to taste
juice of 2 large lemons
6 tablespoons tahini (sesame seed paste)
pinch of ground cumin
1 tablespoon finely chopped parsley

Crush the garlic and salt together. Mix with a little lemon juice and blend with the *tahini*. Add the cumin and remaining lemon juice to form a smooth paste, like peanut butter.

Use more garlic if you want the *tahini* to taste stronger. If it is too thick, reduce it with water. As with *hummus*, a blender is ideal for making *tahini*: the result will be smoother and creamier than if made by hand.

Serve in a bowl, and garnish with the parsley.

Mezze dips made from chick peas, fish roe and sesame seed paste. Hummus (left), taramasalata (centre) and tahini (below).

Dolma *Stuffed Vine Leaves*

Stuffed vine leaves are popular in the eastern Mediterranean countries.

Serves about 10:
50 preserved vine leaves
1 large onion, finely chopped
3 tablespoons olive oil
450 g (1 lb) lean minced lamb
   or beef
100 g (4 oz) long-grain rice
2 tablespoons chopped fresh mint
   (or 2 teaspoons dried)
2 tablespoons chopped fresh dill
   (or 2 teaspoons dried)
salt and black pepper
4 1/2 tablespoons chicken stock
juice of 1-2 lemons
1 lemon, thinly sliced

Cut the stems off the leaves and place them in a large bowl. Pour boiling water over and soak for 20 minutes then ease the leaves apart in the water. Drain, soak briefly in cold water and drain again.

Sauté the onion in the oil until it is soft. Add the meat and cook until it changes colour. Add the rice, herbs and salt and pepper, stirring gently over a low heat until the rice is coated and glazed with the oil.

Add the stock and simmer on a medium heat until the liquid is absorbed. Finally mix in the lemon juice. Set aside and allow to cool.

Line the base of a heavy pan with two or three of the vine leaves. Lay the remainder, vein side up, on a wooden surface and place a teaspoon of the meat mixture in the centre.

Roll up each leaf with the sides neatly tucked in, and stack in layers in the pan. Place slices of lemon between each layer. Place a heatproof dish on top of the leaves to hold them down, pour in water almost to the top, cover with a lid and cook for 30 minutes, or until the rice is tender. The vine leaves should be slightly chewy.

Serve lukewarm, sprinkled with some more lemon juice.

Labneh *Thick Yoghurt*

Serves about 4:
300 ml (½ pint) natural yoghurt
salt, to taste
finely chopped fresh mint, to
garnish
olive oil

Fold a large piece of damp muslin in half, and place over a large bowl. Pour the yoghurt into the centre of the cloth, tie the cloth corners together with string and suspend over the bowl overnight.

Remove from the cloth, tip into another bowl, stir in salt to taste and chill. Garnish with chopped fresh mint and a trickle of olive oil in the centre.

Labneh will keep for one week in a sealed container in the refrigerator. Serve with pita bread as a dip. In many Middle Eastern countries it is eaten with olives for breakfast.

Labneh is a wholesome yoghurt dip.
Muhammara (above) is a hot dip excellent with grilled meats.

Muhammara *Hot Pepper Dip* (picture of page 27)

Serves about 6:
3 medium onions, finely
 chopped
6 1/2 tablespoons olive
 oil
75 g (3 oz) walnut pieces
40 g (1 1/2 oz) fresh
 breadcrumbs blended with
 cold water to a purée
1 1/2 tablespoons paprika (or 1
 teaspoon chilli powder for a
 very hot muhammara) or
 1 small can hot pepper
 purée
a pinch of ground cumin
salt
1 tablespoon pine nuts sautéed
 in a little oil

Using a deep frying pan, sauté the onions gently in the oil until soft and golden. Add the walnuts, the breadcrumb purée, the pepper (or chilli or purée), the cumin and salt to taste. Continue to sauté gently on a low heat until the ingredients are well blended – about 12 minutes.

Remove from the heat, place in a bowl and garnish with the pine nuts.

Muhammara is eaten as a dip with bread. It can also be used as a spicy dip with kebabs, grilled meats and fish. The Lebanese also eat it as a spread on toast.

Falafel *Butter Bean Rissoles*

Serves about 6:
450 g (1 lb) butter beans or chick
 peas
6 spring onions, finely chopped
3 cloves garlic, crushed
6 tablespoons finely chopped
 parsley
1 1/2 teaspoons ground cumin
1 1/2 teaspoons ground coriander
1/2 teaspoon baking powder
salt and cayenne pepper
oil, for deep frying
lemon wedges, to garnish

Soak the beans overnight in plenty of cold water. The next day, drain, and then skin (not necessary for chick peas). Grind in a food processor, or pound in a mortar.

Add all the other ingredients (except for the oil) and blend or pound to a smooth paste-like consistency. Stand uncovered for 15 minutes, then chill. The paste will dry out in the refrigerator and the *falafel* will be easier to handle.

With moistened hands, take small lumps, flatten slightly to form a rissole shape and place on a tray. Prepare the remaining bean mixture in this manner.

Heat 1 cm (½ inch) oil in a deep frying pan and fry the rissoles, turning frequently until they are golden brown. Drain on paper towels and serve garnished with lemon wedges. *Falafel* are eaten with a side dish of *tahini* dip.

Right *Falafel are crunchy spiced bean rissoles. A popular Egyptian snack, they are eaten dipped in tahini.*

Tabbouleh *Lebanese "National" Salad*

Serves 6:

150 g (5 oz) bulghur *(cracked wheat)*
175 g (6 oz) *finely chopped onion*
3½ *tablespoons chopped fresh mint*
8 *tablespoons chopped parsley*
2 *medium tomatoes, diced*
1 x 5 cm (2 inch) *piece, diced cucumber*
salt and pepper to taste
3 *tablespoons olive oil*
3 *tablespoons lemon juice*
black olives, to garnish

Soak the *bulghur* for 1 hour before preparing the salad. Drain it and squeeze out the moisture. Further dry on a cloth.

Place it in a bowl with the finely chopped onion, and mix together, making sure the onion juice penetrates the grains thoroughly. Add the mint, parsley, tomato, cucumber, seasonings, oil and lemon juice, and mix well. Above all, *tabbouleh* should have a distinctive lemony flavour.

Serve the salad chilled, in a glass dish, decorated with a few black olives. *Tabbouleh* is eaten scooped up in bread or, more traditionally in fresh lettuce leaves.

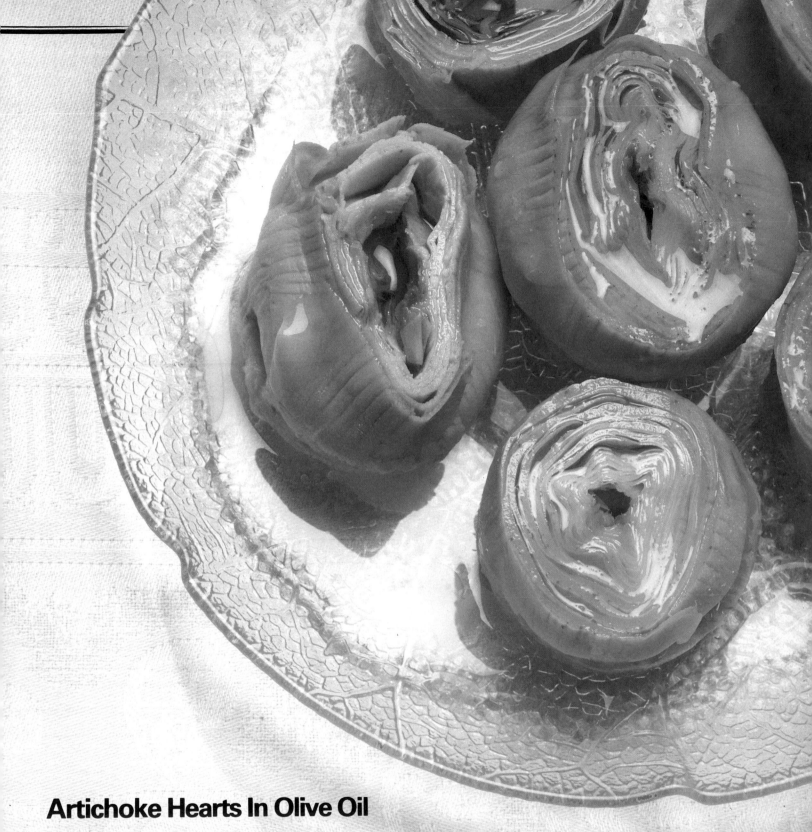

Artichoke Hearts In Olive Oil

Serves 4:
6 small fresh artichokes
6 tablespoons lemon juice
2 cloves garlic, halved
6 tablespoons olive oil
salt and pepper

Remove the stalk and outer leaves of each artichoke and drop the hearts into a bowl of cold water acidulated with a few drops of the lemon juice.

Place the hearts in a heavy pan with 400 ml (14 fl oz) water, half the quantities of lemon juice and olive oil and the garlic. Season with salt and pepper, then bring to the boil. Simmer uncovered until the hearts are tender, about 20–30 minutes.

Remove the hearts from the liquid and cool. Mix the rest of the oil and lemon juice with half the remaining liquid, add more seasoning to taste. Pour over the hearts and chill. Serve cold.

Sanbusak *Stuffed Crescent Pastries*

Makes about 20 sanbusaks:
Pastry
50 g (2 oz) butter
120 ml (4 fl oz) oil
120 ml (4 fl oz) water
1 teaspoon salt
450 g (1 lb) plain flour
egg yolk, or milk to glaze

Sanbusak (or börek in Turkish) are savoury pastries stuffed with meat, spinach or cheese. Serve hot or cold.

To make the pastry, melt the butter gently and pour into a china bowl. Add the oil, water and salt and stir well.

Add the flour, a tablespoonful at a time, mixing in thoroughly. Any lumps will gradually disappear. The consistency is correct when pieces of pastry flake off the sides of the bowl, and you can form a ball of smooth dough in your hands.

While you are stuffing the *sanbusaks*, preheat the oven to 180°C/350°F/Gas Mark 4.

To make a *sanbusak*, break off a walnut-sized piece of pastry, and roll to a circle of about 7.5 cm (3 inches) in diameter. Put a teaspoon of the filling on one-half of the circle, taking care not to over-fill (the mixture expands during the cooking), and fold the other half over the filling.

Close the sides of the pastry well by crimping with your fingers and thumb. Continue until pastry and filling are used up.

Lay each *sanbusak* side by side in a baking dish, glaze with egg yolk or milk, and bake until golden brown – about 30 minutes.

Cheese Filling

225 g (8 oz) Feta cheese
pepper
2 hard boiled eggs, diced
3 tablespoons chopped
  parsley or chives

Mix the ingredients to a paste and stuff the
sanbusak as described. It is not necessary to use
salt with a salty white cheese.

Meat Filling

1 medium onion, finely
  chopped
50 g (2 oz) pine nuts
1 1/2 tablespoons butter
225 g (8 oz) lean minced
  lamb or beef
1/2 teaspoon ground allspice
salt and pepper to taste

Sauté the onion and nuts in the butter until
golden. Add the meat, salt and allspice, and
cook gently until the meat changes colour,
about 12 – 15 minutes. Remove from the pan
and cool. Use to stuff the *sanbusak* as
described.

Spinach Filling

450 g (1 lb) fresh spinach
1 medium onion, finely chopped
olive oil, for frying
salt and white pepper
pinch of paprika
100 g (4 oz) Feta cheese, crumbled

Remove and discard stems and large veins
from the spinach, then wash, drain and chop
the leaves finely.

  Sauté the onion in a little oil until soft and
golden. Add the spinach and seasonings and
cook until tender. Allow to cool, then mix in
the cheese before stuffing the *sanbusaks* as
described.

Kadın Budu *"Lady's Thighs"*

Serves about 4:

450 g (1 lb) lean minced beef or lamb
2 eggs
50 g (2 oz) rice
1 teaspoon oil
1 medium onion, finely chopped
2 1/2 tablespoons finely chopped parsley
salt and pepper
flour, to coat
100 g (4 oz) butter

Knead the meat well in a large bowl, then add one of the eggs, the rice, oil, chopped onion and parsley. Season and mix very well with the meat to form a smooth paste.

With moistened hands, break off lumps and shape into walnut-sized balls. Place in a frying pan with a cup of water and simmer gently for 30 minutes. Drain and cool.

Beat the remaining egg, dip the meat balls in it, then roll them in flour. Fry in the melted butter over a high heat until they are crisp and brown. Keep warm until ready to serve.

Kibbeh Nayé *Raw Seasoned Meat with Bulghur*

Serves about 4:
75 g (3 oz) bulghur *(cracked wheat)*
2 medium onions
450 g (1 lb) top quality minced beef
generous pinch of paprika
salt and freshly ground black pepper, to taste
cayenne pepper, to sprinkle

Wash the *bulghur* and soak in cold water for 2 hours. Squeeze dry in a clean teatowel.

Grate the onion in a food processor, add the meat, *bulghur* and seasonings, and mix to a paste-like consistency.

Take small portions of the *kibbeh* mixture and roll into finger shapes in the palms of your hands. Place on a bed of lettuce leaves and splash with olive oil and lemon juice. Sprinkle with cayenne pepper, if desired.

Kibbeh nayé is the Middle Eastern version of *steak tartare*. To spice it up, you may care to add more Western-style ingredients such as a splash of Worcestershire sauce, Tabasco etc. Other ways of serving it include flattening the mixture in a glass dish and serving with a dish of lettuce leaves to scoop up small portions.

Brains in Lemon and Olive Oil Dressing

Serves 6:
4 sets lambs' brains
4 tablespoons vinegar
1/2 lemon, sliced
1/2 onion, sliced
salt and white pepper, to taste
juice of 1 1/2–2 lemons
4 1/2 tablespoons
*   olive oil*
2 1/2 tablespoons finely chopped
*   parsley*
1/2 clove garlic, crushed

Under a cold tap, remove the brain membranes and clean thoroughly. Put the brains in a pan, add 900 ml (1½ pints) water, the vinegar, lemon and onion slices, and a pinch of salt. Cover and simmer for 15 minutes on a low heat. Do not cook too vigorously or the brains will break. Leave to cool, then drain.

Now cut the brains into quarters. Blend the lemon juice, oil, parsley, garlic and seasonings to taste and pour over the brains. Serve chilled with lemon wedges and garnish of parsley.

Fried Liver

Serves about 4:
225 g (8 oz) lambs' or calves' liver
salt and pepper
1 clove garlic, crushed
pinch of paprika
1 1/2 tablespoons butter
3 tablespoons lemon juice
parsley, to garnish

Soak the liver for 30 minutes in cold, salted water. Remove, pat dry on kitchen paper and cut the slices into thin strips.

Rub the salt, pepper and garlic into the liver strips, then sprinkle with paprika.

Heat the butter, add lemon juice and toss the liver in it over a high heat for about ½ minute each side. Remove to a dish and serve immediately, garnished with the parsley.

Beid Ghanam *Sautéed Lambs' Testicles*

Serves about 4:
about 225 g (8 oz) lambs' testicles
salt
vinegar
lemon and onion slices
1 clove garlic, crushed
100 g (4 oz) butter
1/4 teaspoon mixed herbs
white pepper
juice of 1 lemon
finely chopped parsley, to
*   garnish*

To clean the testicles, first remove the outer skin by slicing the sac and pushing the testicles out. Separate the sac by cutting the connected duct. Discard the sac and rinse the testicles under cold running water. Parboil in salted water (1 tablespoon to 600 ml (1 pint)) for five minutes. Drain, cool, remove any veins and cut into small cubes.

Sauté the crushed garlic in melted butter, then add the herbs, salt and pepper. Toss the testicles lightly in the butter until golden brown. Do not overcook. Finally add the lemon juice and serve hot, garnished with finely chopped parsley.

Chicken Wings with Garlic and Yoghurt

Serves about 4:
8 chicken wings, cut in half
6 tablespoons lemon juice
2 cloves garlic, crushed
1 teaspoon paprika
salt and white pepper
175 ml (6 fl oz) natural yoghurt
parsley, to garnish

Marinate the wings in lemon juice with crushed garlic and seasonings for 1 hour, turning occasionally. Remove and drain.

Mix the yoghurt into the marinade, then brush onto the wings. Place under a medium-hot grill. As the yoghurt dries, brush more on. The wings should become brown and crisp. Serve warm, garnished with parsley.

Fried Mussels

Serves 8-10:
40 large mussels
oil, for deep frying
flour, for coating
lemon wedges and parsley, to
  garnish

White sauce
3 1/2 tablespoons butter
25 g (1 oz) flour
250 ml (8 fl oz) milk
good pinch of mace
salt and pepper

Batter
15 g (1/2 oz) dried yeast
pinch of sugar
1 1/2 tablespoons oil
salt
75 g (3 oz) plain flour, sifted
120 ml (4 fl oz) water, or enough
  to make the consistency of
  single cream

Tarator sauce
2 slices stale white bread,
  soaked in water and
  squeezed dry
65 g (2 1/2 oz) ground almonds or
  pine nuts
2 cloves garlic, crushed
juice of 1 lemon
6 tablespoons olive oil
salt and pepper, to taste

Make the white sauce and the batter first, and allow to stand while you prepare the mussels. For the white sauce, melt the butter in a pan, stir in the flour, and then add the milk gradually, stirring all the time. Add the seasonings, and simmer gently until thick. Cover with greased greaseproof paper and cool. For the batter, dissolve the yeast in a little water with sugar, and leave to froth, about 10 minutes. Mix the yeast, oil and salt into the flour, and add enough water to give the consistency of top of the milk.

Wash the mussels under running water, using a brush and knife to remove beards and any barnacles. Discard any that are open. Make sure any sand or grit is thoroughly rinsed off.

Boil the mussels vigorously in salted water until the shells open, about 5 minutes. Discard any that have not opened. Allow to cool, then remove each mussel from its shell and place on a board. Retain the mussel stock.

Mix the *tarator* sauce ingredients together in a blender, adding enough oil to make a creamy paste.

Heat the oil in a deep pan. Coat each mussel with white sauce, then dip it in the flour and then the batter. Drop into the sizzling oil, and deep-fry until crisp and golden, about 1 minute on a high heat.

Drain and serve immediately on a plate garnished with fresh parsley and lemon wedges with a side dish of *tarator* sauce. Spear the mussels with toothpicks and dip them into the sauce.

In the West mayonnaise or tartare sauce might be served with these fried mussels.

Chicken wings spiked with garlic and lemon can be served hot or cold.

*Mussels fried in batter are
common mezze in Lebanon
and Turkey. Dried fish sticks
are also popular.*

Pickled Chilli Peppers

450 g (1 lb) long mild Chilli
 peppers
1 small dried chilli
1 1/2 tablespoons salt
300 ml (1/2 pint) water
120 ml (4 fl oz) white wine
 vinegar

Prick the peppers all over so that they will absorb the marinade. Pack tightly together in a large glass jar with the chilli. Add salt, water and vinegar, ensuring that there is no air trapped between the peppers.

Seal and store for three weeks by which time the peppers will have softened. Remove the amount required, drain and serve.

Khoubz Arabieh *Arab Bread*

Makes about 20 portions:
600 ml (1 pint) warm water
15 g (1/2 oz) dried yeast
1 tablespoon salt
750 g (1 1/2 lbs) wholemeal flour
1 1/2 tablespoons corn or other
   vegetable oil

No mezze section would be complete without a basic recipe for flat bread.

A cool, crisp accompaniment to Arab bread– salty Feta cheese, black olives and fingers of celery.

Pour the water into a large mixing bowl and sprinkle yeast on the surface. Add the salt and stir until both are dissolved. Gradually add the flour and knead until you have a soft, pliable dough. Add more flour or water as necessary.

Turn the dough ball into a greased bowl, cover with a cloth and allow to rise, about 2 hours. When doubled in size, punch down and divide into 20 equal portions, and roll into ball shapes. Place each ball on a floured work surface, dust with more flour, cover with a cloth and allow to stand a further 15 minutes. Preheat oven to 190°C/375°F/Gas Mark 5.

Next roll each ball flat, about 15 cm (6 inches) in diameter, and place on a greased baking sheet and bake for about 15 minutes until slightly brown and puffy. Serve warm. The pockets can be used for stuffing as in *shawarma*.

Soups

On one of my frequent visits to Jordan, my driver took the twisting King's Highway en route to Petra, via Kerak, a town in the Western escarpment. It was late March and from being a sunny day, the weather suddenly turned black, lightning crackled over the Dead Sea and wind drove sheets of hail against our windscreen. Adeb and I had intended stopping only for a coffee in Kerak, a town known for its lofty, Crusader-built castle, but instead we lingered over a warming bowl of soup. Feast-day Soup is a traditional dish, especially among Jordan's minority Christian community, of whom many live in this area and around Madaba. Dipping in chunks of bread, we found it sustained us for the rest of our journey.

While soups tend to be uncommon in the hot, desert states, they are widely cooked in countries such as Turkey, Syria and Iraq with colder climates. Old Middle Eastern recipe manuals show an infinite number of meat and vegetable soups and many different combinations of both.

Lentil is the most popular, especially in Egypt where *felaheen* may eat it three times a day. The dried pulses that are so widely cultivated in Egypt, Iraq and the Levant – lentils, broad beans, chick peas, split peas and others – make thick, creamy soups or *shorbah* (in Arabic).

Other soups such as vegetable soup are so rich in ingredients that they are almost a stew and, eaten with bread, become a meal in themselves. Common vegetable soups are courgette, carrot and a variety of spinach soups. All use fresh ingredients.

Although I have not given the recipes here, two unusual soups from Egypt and Yemen are *melokhia* and *helba*. Made with a game base and fresh *melokhia* leaves (of the mallow family and resembling mint), the first, from ancient Egypt, is still prepared almost daily by country women, the proportions varying according to the standard of living. *Helba* is a fiery soup served scalding in earthenware bowls. It is eaten daily throughout North Yemen.

Yoghurt soups are a major soup category, the addition of yoghurt or *laban* adding a wholesome taste to any food. Often the yoghurt is only added at the end, merely stirred in and gently heated (as, if boiled, it will curdle). I once enjoyed a splendid yoghurt soup in a small hotel in Konya, the town of whirling dervishes in central Anatolia. The Turks also use prodigious amounts of yoghurt in their cooking; chilled cucumber and yoghurt soup is a perfect start to a lunch on a hot summer's day.

Many people will already know *avgolemono* from a Greek restaurant. The same soup, egg and lemon, or *beid bi limoun* in Arabic, is common in Turkey and Lebanon. A very nourishing soup, especially for anyone who is convalescing, the recipe here is only one of many delicate versions.

Fish soups are popular along the coasts of Turkey, Syria and Lebanon. The recipe included here comes from Izmir, the Turkish port known for its annual September Trade Fair. Beach restaurants in ill-fated Beirut used to serve wonderful *shorbat al samak* made with fresh Mediterranean fish.

The typical sweet and sour marriage of many sophisticated Persian dishes is found in pomegranate soup, an exotic, if time consuming, dish to make. Both Iranians and Iraqis are particularly fond of courgette soup, for which there is a simple recipe that gives wonderful results.

A Western touch with many of these soups might be to garnish them with fried croûtons.

It is the custom for men to shop in Kuwait. The souq is crowded on Thursday morning before Friday, the Muslim holy day.

Egg and Lemon Soup

Serves 6:
1.2 litres (2 pints) homemade chicken stock
salt and pepper, to taste
50 g (2 oz) rice
2 eggs
juice of 1 medium lemon
parsley, to garnish

Heat, but do not boil the chicken stock, then season with salt and pepper. Add the rice and cook slowly until tender, about 10–15 minutes.

Meanwhile, prepare the sauce. Beat the eggs in a small bowl, gradually adding the lemon juice at the same time.

When ready to serve, slowly add the lemon juice mixture to the soup, which should be hot but not boiling (the eggs will curdle if it does boil). Leave to stand for a few minutes before serving, garnished with fresh parsley.

Fish Soup

Serves 6:
1kg (2 lb) white fish
2 medium onions, chopped
4 1/2 tablespoons olive oil
1 small crab, cracked
1 handful mussels, beards
removed and cleaned
2 cloves garlic, crushed
1 leek, white part only,
chopped
1 tablespoon cider vinegar
1 teaspoon turmeric
1/2 teaspoon ground allspice
salt and freshly ground black
pepper, to taste
1 sprig each of fennel and
savory
2 bay leaves
2 egg yolks
juice of lemon
2 tablespoons finely chopped
parsley

Only fresh fish will do for this soup. First sauté the onions in a little of the olive oil. Transfer this to a deep saucepan and add everything except the egg yolks, lemon juice and parsley. Add 1.25 litres (2¼ pints) water and simmer for 1½ hours until a rich broth is obtained.

Strain this broth to get a clear soup, or simply remove any bones, skin and crab-shell. Some cooks put the fish in a cloth and suspend it over a bowl. The juice is

allowed to flow through, and then the cloth wrung out to extract every drop of liquid.

Now beat the egg yolks and slowly add the lemon juice. Take a ladle of the broth and add to this mixture, stirring gently. Finally add the egg and lemon mixture to the saucepan of broth, stir well and simmer on a low heat until ready to serve.

Garnish with the parsley and grind more black pepper over the top.

*Opposite left   Beid bi limoun
or egg and lemon soup.*

*A rich fish soup can be made
with just about any
combination of fresh fish.*

Chilled Cucumber and Yoghurt Soup

1 large cucumber
600 ml (1 pint) natural yoghurt
75 g (3 oz) fresh tomato purée
1 clove garlic, finely chopped
salt to taste
pinch of ground coriander,
mint and paprika, to garnish

Wipe the cucumber clean, but do not peel it. Chop coarsely, sprinkle with salt and allow to stand for 30 minutes. Rinse and drain, and put it in a blender with the remaining ingredients (except for the paprika). Blend until the soup is creamy. Chill.

Serve in chilled bowls, each garnished with a sprinkling of the paprika.

Carrot Soup

Serves 6:
1kg (2 lb) carrots, scraped and
   sliced thinly
50 g (2 oz) butter
salt and pepper
1 teaspoon sugar
1.2 litres (2 pints) homemade
   chicken stock, strained
25 g (1 oz) plain flour
250 ml (8 fl oz) milk
2 egg yolks
finely chopped parsley, to
   garnish

Sauté the carrots in half the butter, then add enough water to cover. Season with the salt and pepper, add the sugar and simmer gently until the carrots are soft. Allow to cool, then put through a blender with the liquid. Now combine the carrot purée and the broth and simmer on a low heat until the purée dissolves into the stock.

Melt the remaining butter in a small pan, add the flour and stir in the milk. When this mixture thickens, take the pan off the heat and add the egg yolks, beating well.

Add this mixture to the basic soup, mix well and return to the stove. Simmer on a low heat – the yolks will curdle if it boils – then serve, garnished with parsley.

Yoghurt Soup

Serves 4:
1 medium onion, finely
   chopped
50 g (2 oz) butter
450 ml (3/4 pint) homemade
   chicken stock, strained
50 g (2 oz) pearl barley, soaked
   overnight
salt and pepper
2 tablespoons finely chopped
   parsley
1 egg
450 ml (3/4 pint) natural yoghurt
2 tablespoons dried mint, crushed

Sauté the onion in the butter until soft and golden. Add the chicken stock and simmer until just below boiling point. Add the drained barley and cook until tender – about 20 minutes – then add seasoning and parsley.

Beat the egg lightly, add it to the yoghurt and blend together well. Then add a little warm stock to the yoghurt and mix. Pour the yoghurt slowly into the stock, and stir over a low heat – do not boil, or the yoghurt will curdle – for about 10–15 minutes. A few drops of fresh lemon juice add zest to this delicious soup. Garnish with the mint.

Above left   *Chilled cucumber soup is ideal for a summer's day.*

Above right   *Cheap and easy to make, carrot soup.*

Below   *The recipe for yoghurt soup has Armenian origins.*

Feast-day Soup

Serves about 4:
*450 g (1 lb) finely minced lean
    lamb*
*salt and freshly ground black
    pepper*
*1 medium onion, very finely
    chopped*
pinch of powdered cinnamon
50 g (2 oz) rice or vermicelli
*600 ml (1 pint) homemade beef
    stock*
juice of 1 lemon
1 tablespoon butter
chopped parsley, to garnish

Season the meat and knead it well. Add the onion and cinnamon and mix thoroughly. With moistened hands, roll the meat into marble–sized balls.

Boil the rice in some water until semi-cooked, then add the broth, meat balls, and lemon juice. Simmer together until the rice is tender, about 15 minutes. Cool.

Reheat just prior to serving, dot with the butter and sprinkle with the parsley. You could add a tablespoon or so of tomato purée to vary this traditional soup from Jordan.

Lentil Soup

Serves 6:
1 large onion, finely chopped
50 g (2 oz) butter
*200 g (7 oz) lentils, soaked
    overnight*
*1.2 litres (2 pints) homemade
    beef stock*
1 teaspoon ground cumin
*salt and freshly ground black
    pepper*
*3 slices white bread, crusts
    removed, diced*
1 clove garlic, crushed
2 tablespoons olive oil
3 tablespoons lemon juice
*finely chopped parsley, to
    garnish*

Sauté the onion gently in half the butter until soft, then add the drained lentils and stir until glazed with the butter. Add the stock, cumin, salt and pepper and simmer until the lentils have almost disintegrated. Raw lentils will take 1½–2 hours. Test the lentils to see whether they are tender, then cool and put the mixture briefly through a blender.

Fry the diced bread (or croûtons) in the remaining butter with the crushed garlic.

Return the soup to the pan, reheat, and bring gently to the boil. Leave to stand for a few minutes before serving, and add the oil and lemon juice. Garnish with the croûtons and a little parsley.

*From Jordan, Feast-day soup
(left) is eaten on auspicious
occasions. Lentil soup (right)
enjoys wide popularity,
especially in Egypt and the
Levant– Lebanon, Syria and
Jordan.*

Vegetable Soup

Serves 6:

1 large onion, finely sliced

3 tablespoons olive oil

450 g (1 lb) stewing beef, cubed

1 large potato, peeled and
    sliced

1 red pepper, seeded and
    sliced

2 carrots, peeled and thinly
    sliced

65 g (2 oz) white cabbage,
    shredded

1.25 litres (2 1/4 pints) homemade
    beef stock

1 tablespoon tomato purée

1 teaspoon dill

salt and pepper

2 tablespoons tarragon
    vinegar

finely chopped parsley, to
    garnish

Using a deep frying pan, sauté the onion gently in the olive oil until it is soft. Add the meat, shaking the pan frequently to prevent the meat from sticking, and cook for 5 minutes. Add the vegetables and cook a further 10 minutes, turning frequently.

Transfer everything to a large, heavy based saucepan and add the stock, tomato purée, dill and seasoning. Simmer gently on a low heat for 1–1½ hours.

Allow to cool, then remove the fat layer from the top. Reheat just before serving, adding the vinegar as a final touch. Garnish with the chopped parsley.

Eaten with chunks of bread, vegetable soup sustains many rural people for an entire day.

Courgette Soup

Serves 4:

3 ½ tablespoons olive oil
450 g (1 lb) courgettes washed,
*   dried and thinly sliced*
2 cloves garlic, crushed
1 large onion, thinly sliced
600 ml (1 pint) homemade
*   chicken stock*
3 tablespoons finely chopped
*   parsley*
salt and freshly ground white
*   pepper*
2 teaspoons lemon juice

Heat the oil, add the courgettes, garlic and onion, and simmer for 10–15 minutes on a low heat. Add the broth, parsley and seasoning and simmer for 15 minutes.

Allow the soup to cool. Stir in the lemon juice and then purée the soup in a blender until almost smooth. Reheat without boiling and serve immediately.

Courgette soup is very nourishing and simple to make.

Tomato Soup

Serves 6:
1 kg (2 lb) medium tomatoes
1 clove garlic, finely chopped
1 medium onion, finely
*   chopped*
600 ml (1 pint) homemade
*   chicken stock*
pinch of ground coriander
pinch of paprika
salt and pepper, to taste
3 1/2 tablespoons olive oil
juice of 1 lemon
finely chopped parsley, to
*   garnish*

Middle Eastern cooking uses only fresh ingredients: tomato soup.

Scald, peel and seed tomatoes, then chop finely. Sauté the garlic, onions, coriander, paprika and seasonings in the olive oil until soft, then add the tomato pulp and cook 5 minutes.

Add the stock (or use half this quantity of stock made up to 600 ml/1 pint with tinned tomato juice, if desired). Cover and simmer 15–20 minutes. Cool the soup, then purée in a blender. Finally stir in the lemon juice, reheat and serve garnished with parsley.

Salads

Harvesting lettuce in the Jordan Valley. Jordan grows most of its food requirements.

Some Middle Eastern countries are as much as two-thirds desert – where it may not rain for years – but revenues from oil and gas deposits, and ingenious irrigation techniques, enable even these places to cultivate vegetables.

Drip irrigation, where each plant has it own "dribble tap", means many of the arid Arabian Gulf states can grow luscious fruits and vegetables. Barren for thousands of years, the desert responds almost magically to water and fertilizers. Sustained on de-salinated water, cucumbers and cabbages grow twice as big as European strains and the tomato yield is prodigious.

In the Fertile Crescent, huge dams irrigate thousands of acres of previously arid countryside. In Syria, the Euphrates Dam has opened the dry eastern province of Raqqa to farming. I met Bedouin who had forsaken their nomadic existence to cultivate lettuces and other seedlings outside their tents.

In Jordan, water from the River Yarmuk is diverted through the East Ghor Canal from which feeder canals irrigate farms along the eastern bank of the River Jordan. The area crops two harvests a year, the entire family, even young children, turning out to help.

Crude farm tools in the National Museum in Baghdad attest to the early skills of Mesopotamian farmers.

Iraq's largest flood control and irrigation system now centres on the Tharthar Reservoir which irrigates the arid plains north west of Baghdad.

But the greatest dam in the Middle East is the 12,230-foot-long Aswan Dam, in Egypt. The dam has made possible perennial irrigation all along the Nile Valley.

The Arab's fascination with water and his ability to utilize even the smallest amounts, dates back some 3,000 years to when the ancient Egyptians built a vast dam across Wadi Gerrawi. Then, using neither mortar nor mechanization, the Sabaean Tribe in Southern Arabia built the giant Marib Dam in what is now known as North Yemen. Ancient texts say that the creation of the dam turned the district into a paradise. Strabo writes of abundant fruits and of great flocks of sheep in the meadows. The collapse of the dam inundated hundreds of miles of farmland and today Marib has been overtaken by seas of drifting sand, a wall and sluice gate being the only evidence of the dam's existence.

On the barren central plateau of Iran, farmers have for centuries cultivated by means of ingenious subterranean canals, or *kanats*, linking the strings of wells. Similar *falaj* or underground irrigation channels are found in al-Buraimi Oasis on the border of Abu Dhabi and the Sultanate of Oman.

So while some countries are still far from being self-sufficient, it is incorrect to only associate dates with the Arab World. Some of the sweetest, crispest salads I have ever eaten have been in the Middle East.

Salads like *tabbouleh* often come as a starter. Otherwise, a fresh salad is invariably served with the main course.

As its name implies, *salata Arabieh* belongs to no particular country, but I always associate it with Lebanon. The freshly grilled fish, or charcoal broiled kebabs always arrived with a bowl of blood red tomatoes, peppermint green cucumbers and tangy onions from the Bekaa Valley, all shiny and inviting under a dressing of garlic, lemon juice and olive oil.

Fattouche, a popular Syrian peasant salad, uses crumbled bread as a variation on the theme. Additional flavours may include chopped fresh mint, parsley and coriander.

The recipe for tomato and coriander salad comes from Yemen, where local cooks have devised all kinds of highly original cold sauces and dips. I am partial to just a plain tomato and onion salad drenched in equal quantities of oil and lemon juice. White cheese, local bread and a tomato and onion salad became a favourite lunch when I stayed at the Winter Palace Hotel overlooking the Nile at Luxor in Egypt.

The use of yoghurt in salads is common in Middle Eastern cuisines, especially in Turkey and Jordan. Cucumber, nut and yoghurt salad is a wonderful summer starter. Another Turkish dish, aubergine salad, is one of my favourites. Cooked spinach also enjoys a close affinity with yoghurt, either plain or with garlic. Garlic, of course, is very much prized in the Middle East.

Kidney Bean Salad

Serves 4-6:
*400 g (14 oz) dried kidney
    beans
juice of 1 1/2 –2 lemons
4 1/2 tablespoons olive oil
salt and black pepper
1 green pepper, chopped
6 spring onions, finely
    chopped
1 tablespoon chopped parsley*

Soak the beans overnight in plenty of cold water, then wash and drain. Boil fast for 15 minutes, then simmer for 1½–2 hours until tender.

Prepare the dressing by mixing together the lemon juice, olive oil, salt and pepper.

Pour over the beans, then mix in the green pepper, onions and parsley.

Line a bowl with lettuce leaves and tip in the bean salad. Garnish with a little more parsley.

Fattouche

Serves 4-6:

1 stale pita bread
225 g (8 oz) coarsely chopped
    onion
4 spring onions, coarsely
    chopped (optional)
1 round lettuce, shredded
4 tablespoons finely chopped
    parsley
1 medium cucumber, coarsely
    chopped
4 medium tomatoes, coarsely
    chopped
1 tablespoon dried mint
juice of 2 large lemons
6 tablespoons olive oil
2 cloves garlic, crushed
salt and pepper, to taste

Break the
bread into small
pieces and put in
a large mixing bowl.
Add the chopped
onions, spring onions,
lettuce, parsley, cucumber,
tomatoes and mint. Mix well, then
leave the bread to absorb the juices,
about 10 minutes.

    Now make a dressing with the lemon
juice, olive oil and garlic. Season with salt
and black pepper and pour over the salad
mixture. Toss well and chill before serving.

Salata Arabieh

Serves 8:
6 medium tomatoes, diced
1 large cucumber, peeled and
*   diced*
2 medium onions, finely
*   chopped*
2 cloves garlic, finely chopped
1 medium green pepper,
*   seeded and diced (optional)*
4 tablespoons chopped fresh
*   mint*
4 tablespoons finely chopped
*   fresh parsley*
juice of 1 1/2–2 lemons
4 1/2 tablespoons olive oil
salt and freshly ground black
*   pepper*

Combine all the vegetables
in a bowl. Mix the remaining
ingredients together and pour
over the vegetables. Toss very well
and chill before serving with pita bread.

Cucumber and Raisin Salad with Yoghurt

Serves about 4:
2 medium cucumbers
salt and freshly ground white
  pepper
175 ml (6 fl oz) natural yoghurt
40 g (1 1/2 oz) raisins
25 g (1 oz) chopped walnuts
2 spring onions; finely chopped
pinch of ground cumin
1 1/2 tablespoons chopped fresh
  mint

Slice cucumber, sprinkle with salt and leave
to drain in a colander for 30 minutes.
   Combine the yoghurt, raisins, walnuts,
spring onions, cumin, salt and pepper in a
bowl. Add the cucumber and mix well.
Finally add the mint and chill prior to serving.

Aubergine Salad

Serves 6:
3 medium aubergines
salt
6 tablespoons oil
3 cloves garlic, crushed
freshly ground black pepper
120 ml (4 fl oz) natural
  yoghurt
pinch each of paprika and
  cumin

Cut the aubergines into 5 mm (1/4 inch) thick
slices. Sprinkle with salt and leave for 30
minutes, weighted down with a flat dish to
help remove the bitter juices. Rinse the
aubergine slices and pat dry on kitchen paper.
   Sauté the slices in hot oil until they are
brown on both sides. Drain on paper towels.
   Mix the garlic, salt and pepper into the
yoghurt. Arrange the aubergine slices in
layers in a flat serving dish and coat well with
the yoghurt. Sprinkle with the paprika, chill
and serve.

Spinach Salad

Serves 4:
450 g (1 lb) fresh spinach
175 g (6 fl oz) natural yoghurt
1 clove garlic, crushed
pinch of cumin
salt and pepper

Clean the fresh spinach under running water
and remove the stems and any large veins.
Chop the leaves and simmer in their own
juices until tender, about 20 minutes. Cool.
   Blend the yoghurt with the garlic, cumin
and seasonings, add to the spinach and mix
well. Chill until ready to serve.

Laced with yoghurt,
cucumber (above left),
aubergine (above right) and
spinach (below) salads are
especially popular in Turkey
and Iran.

Tomato and Coriander Salad

Serves 4:
6 firm, ripe, medium tomatoes
1/2 bunch fresh coriander
   leaves, chopped
pinch of paprika
salt and freshly ground black
   pepper
2 1/2 tablespoons olive oil
juice of 1 lemon

Scald, peel and slice the tomatoes into a bowl.
Sprinkle with the chopped coriander leaves.
   Combine the paprika, salt, pepper, oil and
lemon juice, and beat vigorously. Pour over
the tomatoes, then chill. Remove from the
refrigerator 10 minutes before serving.

Green Pepper Salad

Serves 4:
4 medium green peppers
juice of 1 1/2–2 lemons
4 1/2 tablespoons olive oil
dash of vinegar
1 clove garlic, crushed
salt, to taste
black olives, to garnish

Quarter the green peppers lengthwise, and
remove the seeds. Char under the grill until
the edges are brown and crisp. Allow to cool.
   Make the dressing by mixing together the
remaining ingredients, then pour over the
peppers. Mix well, and garnish with one or
two black olives.

Potato Salad

Serves 4-6:
1 kg (2 lbs) new potatoes,
   scrubbed
good pinch of cumin
4 1/2 tablespoons olive oil
juice of 1 1/2–2 lemons
3 cloves garlic, crushed
salt and pepper
3 1/2 tablespoons finely chopped
   spring onions
4 tablespoons finely chopped
   parsley

Boil the potatoes until they are just tender.
Allow to cool a little, then peel and cut into
uniform chunks. Sprinkle with cumin.
   Prepare the dressing by mixing together
the oil, lemon juice, garlic, salt and pepper.
Pour over the potatoes. Toss well, chill
until required, and serve sprinkled
with the spring onions and
parsley.

Above right   *Green
pepper or fil-fil salad. Below
left   Tomato and coriander
salad from North Yemen.
Below right   Potato salad.*

French Bean, Leek and Asparagus Salad

Serves 4:
450 g (1 lb) prepared vegetables
  (see method)
salt and freshly ground black
  pepper
1 clove garlic, crushed
4 1/2 tablespoons olive oil
juice of 1 1/2–2 lemons

This salad can be made with any variety of green beans, leeks or asparagus. Top, tail and slice the beans if large; wash and slice the leeks; scrape and trim the asparagus stalks.

Cook each vegetable in a little salted water until barely tender, then drain and mix the remaining ingredients together and pour over the vegetables.

For a Western touch, garnish the leeks and the asparagus with chopped parsley and diced hard-boiled egg.

Vegetables and Rice

While the Western vogue for vegetarian cooking has only recently elevated vegetables to "main course" status, vegetables have a historically important position on a Middle Eastern menu. A frequently quoted saying during Abbasid times was: "A table without vegetables is like an old man devoid of wisdom."

Many dishes such as vegetable casserole are meals in themselves. So is stuffed aubergine, a great favourite of Abbasid society, the Caliph Wathiq being reportedly so fond of aubergines that he ate forty at a time. Iraqis transform the humble potato with a minced meat and pine nut filling, while the stuffed tomatoes of Egypt and the Levant have no equal.

While many Middle Eastern cities today have large, Western-style supermarkets, people still turn to the traditional *souqs* for buying fresh vegetables. Store owners display an artistic bent with colourful arrangements of polished tomatoes, shiny courgettes, red and green peppers and purple aubergines. It is unthinkable not to be able to select your own vegetables, which are hunted down as soon as the *souq* opens. Usually the cook or a servant does the shopping, but in some countries it might be the grandmother with one of the servant's sons to carry her basket.

I especially remember an old Palestinian lady, possibly blind, groping slowly through the vegetable market in East Jerusalem. No doubt she knew her way and was probably a familiar figure, small, wrinkled and wearing a long, black robe. Stopping outside one shop, she felt around the display, then held up a smooth skinned aubergine, handing her purse trustingly to the owner for him to extract payment. While waiting, she popped a grape into her mouth; then smiling like a guilty child, she continued her shopping. I watched her buying a lettuce, lemons and bundles of coriander before losing sight of her in the crowds.

In conservative Arab states such as Qatar and Kuwait, it is common for men to do the shopping. By contrast, in Sana'a, well veiled women sell onions, carrots, tomatoes and other vegetables coaxed from the rocky soil.

The most commonly used Middle Eastern vegetables – courgettes, peppers, spinach and so on – are available in Britain. If you have trouble finding others such as okra, try an Indian shop. Always bring home parsley to garnish dishes, and when cooking the Middle Eastern way, never be without a lemon.

Several recipes in this chapter are ideal for vegetarians: the popular *Imam bayıldı* (or swooning Imam), cabbage rolls, okra in oil and bean stew could make an entire buffet. Iran's contribution is an unusual combination of herbs and nuts in an omelette. Spinach is supposed to be native to Iran, but the recipe for spinach pie comes from Turkey, a delicious party dish which can be eaten hot or cold.

Wheat and rice are the main grains used in Middle Eastern cooking. Cracked wheat, or *bulghur,* is more usually

Right *A vegetable market in Dubai. Desert irrigation schemes enable many of the Gulf States to grow excellent vegetables.*

encountered in minced meat dishes, but it can be eaten plain with butter, topped with a fresh tomato purée or garlic flavoured yoghurt with black pepper.

Rice is the basic dish throughout the Middle East: *roz* to the Arabs, *pilav* (cooked with other ingredients) in Turkey and *chelo* (steamed) or *polo* (cooked with other ingredients) in Iran. Basmati rice, which resembles the high grade Southern rice, is preferred, often coloured with saffron or turmeric. A common way of serving it is in a ring garnished with a sauce and nuts. Meats and fish are frequently served on a bed of rice, a good example being the Bedouin whole roast lamb. Following a visit to Iran in 1971, I encountered *chelo*, a rice so subtle that I tend to make it to this day, the exception being saffron rice to serve with fish.

Last, but vital to millions of poorer people in the Middle East, are the dishes based on dried beans and peas: the bean dish, *foul medames*, is almost the national dish of Egypt. Most bean and lentil recipes are geared to peasant tastes – chick peas have already appeared in the guise of *hummus*, and there are recipes for lentil soup and lamb and chick pea casserole in the meat section.

We know that Middle Eastern cooks use a great deal of yoghurt. Natural, or spiked with garlic, it can be served with fried, sautéed or baked vegetables. Lemon juice is routinely used to heighten the flavour of many vegetable dishes such as cabbage rolls or baked aubergine with cumin.

Batata Charp *Stuffed Potatoes*

Serves 4-6:
8 medium potatoes
1 egg
1 1/2 tablespoons cornflour
salt and pepper

Filling
1 medium onion, finely
    chopped
3 tablespoons butter
pinch each of paprika,
    ground cumin and allspice
225 g (8 oz) lean minced
    beef
250 ml (8 fl oz) cooking oil

First make the filling. Sauté the onion in the butter until golden and soft. Add the seasonings, then the meat. Cook for about 5 minutes until it changes colour. Remove and set aside.

Peel and boil the potatoes. Mash well in a large bowl then add the egg, cornflour, salt and pepper. Mix in very thoroughly. With moist hands break off a lump the size of a golf ball. Roll it in your hands, then flatten on your work surface and make a small hollow in the top. Fill this with a teaspoonful of the meat mixture and close the edges. Roll the potato ball around in your hand to ensure the meat is well sealed inside. Repeat this procedure until all the meat and potato is used up. Refrigerate the potato balls for at least 1 hour.

Heat the cooking oil in a deep saucepan. When the oil is sizzling, gently lower a potato ball into the saucepan and cook quickly, turning on all sides until it is a golden brown. Cook each ball separately and be careful it does not break.

This amount makes about 15 potato balls. Serve with a chopped Arab salad, bread and a *labneh* dip.

Stuffed Tomatoes

Serves 2-4:
4 large firm tomatoes
salt and pepper
1 onion, finely chopped
4 1/2 tablespoons olive oil
75 g (3 oz) rice
pinch sugar
1 tablespoon currants
1 tablespoon pine nuts,
    chopped
1 tablespoon finely chopped
    mint
1 tablespoon finely chopped
    parsley

Select tomatoes of a uniform size. Carefully slice off the tops and set aside. Scoop out the pulp with a small spoon, removing any hard core, then chop the pulp. Sprinkle the inside of each tomato case with salt and pepper, and leave upside down to drain.

Sauté the onion gently in the olive oil until soft and golden. Add the tomato pulp, and the remaining ingredients, and simmer on a low heat for 3 minutes. Add 250 ml (8 fl oz) water and cook gently until the rice softens, about 10 minutes. Preheat oven to 180°C/350°F/Gas Mark 4.

Allow the mixture to cool, then spoon it into each tomato case, leaving enough room for the rice to swell. Top each tomato with its own "lid", and arrange side by side in an oiled baking dish. Brush each with a little extra oil and bake for 30 minutes.

Imam Bayıldı *Baked Aubergine*

Serves 6:
3 medium aubergines
salt
175 g (6 oz) chopped onion
6 tablespoons olive oil
3 cloves garlic, crushed
1 small red pepper, seeded
*   and diced*
5-6 medium tomatoes,
*   skinned and finely chopped*
1 1/2 tablespoons pine nuts,
*   chopped*
1 1/2 tablespoons raisins, chopped
1/2 teaspoon cayenne pepper
juice of 1 large lemon

Cut the aubergines in half lengthways. Using a serrated spoon, or similar, scoop out the flesh, being careful not to puncture the skin. Leave a case about 5 mm (¼ inch) thick. Chop and salt the pulp, place in a colander, and leave to drain for 1 hour. Rinse under cold running water then pat dry with kitchen paper. Rinse and dry the cases as well.

Fry the onion in some of the oil until it softens. Mix in the garlic and cook a further 3 minutes. Stir in the aubergine pulp, the pepper and the tomatoes, and cook over a medium heat until the pepper softens and most of the liquid has evaporated. Remove the pan from the heat and mix in the pine nuts, raisins, salt and cayenne pepper.

Preheat the oven to 180°C/350°F/Gas Mark 4, and put the remaining oil in an ovenproof baking dish. Arrange the aubergine cases in it, in a close fitting layer. Fill each case with the stuffing and sprinkle with lemon juice. Gently add boiling water down one side of the baking dish to come about half-way up the aubergines. Cover with foil and bake in the oven for about 1 hour. Remove the dish when the cases are tender, and allow the aubergines to cool in the sauce.

When the aubergines are cold, drain off excess liquid and trickle a little extra olive oil over the cases. Chill until about 10 minutes before serving.

Stuffed vegetables are a feature of Middle Eastern cooking. Stuffed potatoes (above left) are a favourite in Iraq. Stuffed tomatoes (above right) may be eaten either hot or cold. Stuffed aubergine (below), here ready for the oven, is a medieval Turkish dish.

Baked Aubergine with Cumin

Serves 4:

1 kg (2 lb) medium aubergines
6 cloves garlic, crushed
4 1/2 tablespoons olive oil
1 teaspoon paprika
1 heaped teaspoon ground
  cumin
2 pinches cayenne pepper
salt
lemon juice

Preheat the oven to 220–230°C/425–450°F/ Gas Mark 7–8.

Wash and dry the aubergines. Slit the skin in several places to prevent them bursting, then steam until tender, about 30–40 minutes (in a pressure cooker, about 12–15 minutes). Allow to cool, then cut each aubergine into three lengthways. Sprinkle with the garlic.

Heat the oil in an ovenproof dish in the oven. Put the aubergines in and sprinkle with paprika, cumin, cayenne pepper and a little

salt. Bake for 5 minutes.

Just before serving, sprinkle with a few drops of fresh lemon juice.

Baked aubergine sprinkled
with cumin is a common
Middle Eastern recipe. Dip
Arab bread into the sauce.

Cabbage Rolls

Serves 8-10:
20 cabbage leaves

Stuffing
100 g (4 oz) rice
3 tablespoons olive oil
*2 medium onions, finely
    chopped*
2 cloves garlic, crushed
1 1/2 tablespoons pine nuts
*225 g (8 oz) lean minced
    lamb or beef*
*3 medium tomatoes, finely
    chopped*
1/2 teaspoon cumin
1/2 teaspoon ground allspice
1 tablespoon dried mint
lemon juice, to sprinkle

First make the stuffing. Cook the rice in boiling water for about 8 minutes. Drain. Sauté the onions, garlic and pine nuts until golden, then add the minced meat; stir well and cook until it changes colour. Add tomatoes, mint, cumin and allspice and simmer the mixture for a further 5 minutes. Keep warm.

Choose large, whole, fresh cabbage leaves. Plunge into boiling salted water to make them pliable, then spread on a wooden board and cut out the cores. Place a portion of stuffing on each leaf and roll into a neat

packet. Preheat the oven to 180°C/350°F/Gas Mark 4.

Place the rolls close together in a shallow casserole dish and add enough salted water (or stock) to almost cover. Make sure they are tightly packed or they might unwrap. Cover and cook for about 40 minutes, or until tender.

Serve hot sprinkled with fresh lemon juice, or a sauce made from fresh tomatoes and cream– as preferred.

Stuffed and spiced, the humble cabbage is elevated to almost regal status.

French Bean Stew

Serves 6:

1 kg (2 lb) French beans

Tomato Sauce

3 cloves garlic, crushed
1/2 teaspoon ground coriander
2 tablespoons olive oil
2 medium onions, chopped
1 1/2 tablespoons tomato purée
6 medium tomatoes, skinned
1 tablespoon chopped parsley
salt and white pepper
1/2 teaspoon paprika
juice of 1 lemon

First, prepare the tomato sauce. Sauté the garlic and coriander in the oil, then add the onions and cook the mixture for 10 minutes. Add the tomato purée, tomatoes and parsley and crush and blend into a purée. Mix in the salt, pepper, paprika and lemon juice and simmer uncovered for 15 minutes. Stir frequently to make a rich, aromatic sauce.

Trim the beans as necessary and place in a large saucepan with the sauce and enough water to barely cover. Simmer until tender (about 15 minutes).

If you prefer your beans *al dente*, remove after 10 minutes and set aside while you reduce the sauce to a thicker consistency. Return the beans and reheat to serve.

Courgettes with Tomatoes

Serves 4:

1 kg (2 lb) courgettes
2 cloves garlic, crushed
pinch of ground coriander
3 tablespoons olive oil
6 medium tomatoes
salt and black pepper
1 1/2 tablespoons chopped parsley

Wash and dry the courgettes, and slice into moderately thick rounds.

Sauté the garlic and coriander in the oil, then add the courgette slices. Cook gently for

about 10 minutes, turning frequently.

Add the tomatoes, peeled and chopped, salt, pepper and parsley, and simmer until cooked, about 20 minutes. Serve hot.

Okra Stew

Serves 4:
6 medium tomatoes, sliced
450 g (1 lb) fresh okra
cider vinegar
3 cloves garlic, crushed
2 medium onions, finely
  chopped
1 teaspoon coriander
1 1/2 tablespoons olive oil
salt and pepper
1 tablespoon tomato
  purée
ground cumin
juice of 1 lemon

French bean stew (below left), courgettes with tomatoes (below right) and okra or bamieh (right) are favourite vegetable dishes in the Middle East.

Scald, skin and slice the tomatoes. Wash and cut off the okra stems, taking care not to puncture the pods. Soak the okra for 30 minutes in vinegar to prevent them becoming sticky during cooking. Drain and rinse under running water. Preheat oven to 180°C/350°F/ Gas Mark 4.

Sauté the garlic, coriander and onions in the olive oil until soft. Place half in a greased flameproof casserole, and top with a layer of sliced tomato. Make second layers of onion and tomato, then arrange the okra on top. Season and top with the remaining tomatoes.

Mix tomato purée with a little water, pour over the vegetables, then add enough water to almost cover them. Add a good pinch of cumin and cook for 10 minutes over a high heat.

Remove from heat, add lemon juice and bake until the okra are tender (about 1 hour). By now the liquid will have reduced by a third.
Serve hot in the casserole dish.

Herb and Nut Omelette

Serves 4:
3 tablespoons butter
6 spring onions, finely
* chopped*
2 lettuce leaves, finely chopped
1 teaspoon dried dill (or 2 1/2
* tablespoons fresh dill)*
4 tablespoons
* chopped parsley*
8 eggs
saffron to colour, or 1/4 teaspoon
* turmeric*
a pinch of cinnamon
salt and pepper
a pinch of bicarbonate of soda
25 g (1 oz) raisins, roughly chopped
25 g (1 oz) chopped walnuts

Melt half the butter in an ovenproof frying pan. Add the spring onions, lettuce, dill and parsley and sauté until the spring onions are transparent. Add the remaining butter and allow to melt.

Heat the oven to 180°C/350°F/Gas Mark 4.

Beat the eggs well, then add saffron (or turmeric), cinnamon, salt and pepper and bicarbonate of soda. Stir in the raisins and nuts. Pour this mixture into the frying pan but do not stir. Transfer to the preheated oven and bake until golden and set.

Serve immediately, either alone or with a tomato salad.

Ideal for vegetarians, a magically flavoured herb and nut omelette from Iran.

Baked Squash in Tahini Sauce

Serves 4-6:

4 medium yellow squash
50 g (2 oz) butter
3 medium onions, finely
 chopped
4 cloves garlic, crushed
pepper
1/2 teaspoon ground coriander
1/2 teaspoon paprika
1/4 teaspoon ground cinnamon
450 g (1 lb) lean minced lamb
 or beef
salt
4 tablespoons tahini
 (sesame seed paste)
5 tablespoons lemon juice, or more
50 g (2 oz) pine nuts (or walnuts)

Peel the squash and slice into rounds about 1 cm (½ inch) thick. Sauté in the butter until almost cooked and golden brown. Set aside.

In the same pan, sauté the onions and half of the crushed garlic. Season with pepper, coriander, paprika and cinnamon, then add the meat and cook until lightly brown. Add salt.

Line a greased casserole dish with a layer of closely packed squash, spread the meat mixture over it, then layer with remaining squash.

Blend the *tahini,* lemon juice, remaining garlic and salt to taste in a bowl. Blend to the consistency of top of the milk, adding more lemon juice if necessary. Pour this into the casserole and bake at 190°C/375°F/ Gas Mark 5 until the top turns a golden brown (about 40 minutes).

Baked squash with tahini is a
tasty recipe from Lebanon.

Turkish Vegetable Casserole

Serves 6-8:

1 medium aubergine, sliced
salt
4 medium okra, about 7.5 cm
   (3 inches) long
2 medium onions, chopped
1 green pepper, seeded
   and chopped
4 medium courgettes, unpeeled
   and coarsely chopped
100 g (4 oz) beans
100 g (4 oz) green peas
450 g (1 lb) potatoes, peeled and
   cubed
4 cloves garlic, crushed
1 bunch of parsley, finely
   chopped
2 teaspoons paprika
1 heaped teaspoon ground
   cumin
5-6 medium tomatoes, peeled
   and sliced
5-7 tablespoons olive oil
1 teaspoon sugar

Soak the aubergine slices in salted water for 30 minutes; remove and drain well. Prepare okra as for Okra Stew (page 71).

Sauté the onion in a little of the oil until soft and golden. Transfer to a casserole dish and add the remaining vegetables, except the tomatoes. Add the garlic, parsley and all the seasonings, 450 ml (15 fl oz) water (or stock) and most of the olive oil. Mix together, then add the tomatoes and dribble in the remaining olive oil. Finally flatten the vegetables down with a wooden spoon. Preheat the oven to 190°C/375°F/Gas Mark 5.

Cover and bake for about 1 hour or until the vegetables are tender. Remove the casserole, add salt to taste and the sugar, stir well and cook a further 15–20 minutes.

Serve the vegetable casserole with bread as a hot dip. The Turks also like *turlu guvec* cold.

Rich Turkish vegetable casserole or turlu guvec.

Far right *Spinach pie is a Turkish favourite. It makes an excellent party dish eaten hot, or cold.*

Spinach Pie

Serves 6-8:
12 sheets filo pastry
300 ml (¹/₂ pint) olive oil

Filling
1.25 kg (2¹/₂ lb) fresh spinach
    (or thawed frozen spinach)
salt and pepper
175 g (6 oz) onions, chopped
1¹/₂ tablespoons butter
4 large eggs, beaten
225 g (8 oz) Feta cheese, crumbled
    (or Parmesan and Feta mixed)
2 teaspoon dried dill
1 heaped teaspoon paprika

First prepare the filling. If using fresh spinach, wash it, remove the stalks and any large veins, and cut the leaves into thin strips. Sprinkle with salt and leave for 1 hour. Then rub the leaves and squeeze out all the liquid. Follow package instructions for frozen spinach.

Sauté the onions in the butter until transparent. Add onions, beaten eggs, cheese, dill and paprika to the spinach and mix well. Add salt and pepper to taste.

Heat oven to 180°C/350°F/Gas Mark 4. Grease a 25 x 30 cm (10 x 12 inch) baking dish.

Brush one side of one sheet of the pastry with oil and lay it in the tin – which it will

overlap. Brush five more sheets individually with oil and place on top. Now place the spinach filling on this and trickle 2 tablespoons olive oil over it.

Bring the overlapping pastry up over the filling. Cut the last six sheets to the size of the tin, brush them individually with oil and lay them on top.

Score the top into squares and sprinkle with water to prevent the edges curling. Bake in the oven until the top is a golden brown, about 30–45 minutes.

Saffron Rice

Serves 4:
350 g (12 oz) rice
3 tablespoons pine nuts
2 tablespoons olive oil
3 medium onions, finely
  chopped
2 tablespoons raisins
1 teaspoon salt
enough saffron to colour, or ½
  teaspoon turmeric

Wash and soak the rice for 2 hours. Rinse in a sieve under running water until clear, then drain. Brown the pine nuts in the oil, then add the onions and sauté them until soft and golden. Divide this mixture in half.

Add the raisins and one half of the mixture to the rice together with the salt and saffron or turmeric. Bring 700 ml (1¼ pints) of water to the boil, add the rice etc., and stir for 1 minute over a medium heat. Reduce the heat, and simmer until the water is absorbed, about 15–20 minutes. Stir in the rest of the onions and pine nuts, mix well, and serve immediately.

Plain Pilaf Rice

Serves 2-3:
225 g (8 oz) long-grain rice
1 ½ tablespoons butter or oil
salt

Wash the rice in a sieve under running water until it is clear. Soak for 2 hours in cold water, then drain.

Boil 300 ml (½ pint) water, and add the butter (or oil), salt and rice. Bring back to the boil, stir well, cover and cook for 15–20 minutes. To colour, add several strands of saffron, or ½ teaspoon of turmeric, to the water.

Chelo *Persian Steamed Rice*

Serves 4:
350 g (12 oz) Basmati rice
3 tablespoons melted butter
1 tablespoon salt
1 egg yolk, to serve (optional)

Wash rice in boiling water then soak in salted water for 6 hours. Rinse the rice in a sieve under running water until it is clear. Place in a pan, add a pinch of salt, cover with boiling water and cook vigorously for 10 minutes. Wash and drain again.

To steam the rice, heat 120 ml (4 fl oz) cold water and 1 tablespoon butter in a saucepan. Add the rice, smoothing it flat. Fold a clean teatowel in half and place it over the top of the saucepan then cover with the lid. The teatowel will trap and absorb the steam, helping the rice to remain fluffy.

After 15 minutes, the rice should be ready. Trickle the remaining butter over it and serve. Iranians serve an egg yolk in a hollow made in each portion of *chelo*.

Three different rices – chelo or Persian steamed rice (centre), plain boiled rice pilaf (top) and saffron rice (right) for serving with fish. A raw egg yolk, butter and spices are mixed into the chelo for eating with kebabs in Iran.

Meat

My first taste of Middle Eastern cookery came in Aden, now capital of the Democratic Republic of South Yemen. In 1963, a passenger liner bearing me and several hundred other young Australians called at Aden on her three and a half week voyage to Europe.

Tired of shipboard food, we had streamed ashore in search of something fresh when the odour of grilling meat drew me into a small restaurant. Surrounded by curious men, I had my first taste of *kebabs* and while I have subsequently eaten them from Casablanca to Peshawar, I still remember this simple dish, and the cook polishing my knife and fork on his apron.

Shish kebab, to use the full name, is credited with being a Turkish creation. The story goes that, obliged to camp out during the Ottoman conquests, Turkish soldiers adopted the habit of cooking skewered meat – goat, lamb, gazelle and so on – over an open fire outside their tents. In fact, it could just as easily have been devised by invading Persian or Mongol tribes.

On the subject of *kebabs*, the most important considerations are to purchase a good cut of meat and to marinate it for at least three to four hours. I usually mix a marinade made from the juice of two large onions, 6 tablespoons olive oil, a teaspoon of oregano, a pinch of cayenne pepper, plus salt and freshly ground black pepper, and refrigerate the meat in it overnight in a covered non-metal bowl. When barbecuing *kebabs*, or any other meat, fish or poultry, wait until the charcoal has ceased smoking before you start cooking. Under the grill, cook quickly under a high heat to seal the juices, then brown the outside. The cooking time will depend on how well you like your meat done.

The ways of cooking meat in the Middle East are basically the same

Sizzling kebabs cooked at a roadside stall by the Desert Highway in Jordan.

Döner kebap has travelled the world with Turkish migrants. The cooked lamb is carved into a pocket of bread with salad and spices.

as in the West: grilling or barbecuing, stewing and roasting. Minced meat dishes are very popular in the Levant and Syria in particular, where women vie with each other to produce the finest *kibbeh*.

The Arabs tend to eat more barbecued meats, such as *kebabs* and lamb roasted on a spit. *Yaknéh*, or meat and vegetable stews, are common in the Levant. The Yemenis, too, are fond of stews, a popular ingredient being okra; okra (*bamieh*) is also a traditional dish in Egypt. Some Middle Eastern stews have an earthy, rather peasant-type texture – like the lamb and chick pea casserole. The more refined Persian taste, which permeates all types of local cooking, is found in the veal and prune casserole dish, a fascinating blend of "sweet and sour" ingredients.

Stews are normally simmered a long time on the stove. Alternatively, if the ingredients have been sealed by frying, or sautéeing, they are baked in the oven.

With people always running in and out of the kitchen, and servants, grandmothers and friends to help, there is always someone to watch a meal cooking in a Middle Eastern household.

So often discarded in the West, bones are prized for the marrow, a cracked bone is often added to stews for extra richness. Unlike meat for grilling, you can buy cheaper cuts for a stew. Searing meats in oil, or butter, traps the juices and adds a richer colour to the dish. Simmering the meat, as in many Persian recipes, makes for a light, almost insipid looking stew which is then enriched with spices, nuts and fruits. Most Middle Eastern cooks find it difficult to be precise about quantities; they tend to cook by heart with constant tastings and adjustings.

Organs are revered as we have seen with brains, liver and testicles in the chapter on *mezze*. I have marvellous memories of brains served in the Oriental buffet at the Hilton Hotel in al-Ain, the large oasis town in inland Abu Dhabi. I have eaten kidneys just about everywhere. Up early to photograph Shibam, a mountain town outside Sana'a, my driver and I had liver for breakfast. Served with a bowl of *foul* and flat wholemeal bread, it is a speciality of Yemeni

mountain towns on market day. Lamb's testicles are more rarely available. I have only ever eaten them in Lebanon and in Lebanese restaurants in London. They are of a taste and texture similar to sweetbreads and you should have your butcher prepare them as they are rather messy.

Lamb or mutton is the most commonly used meat throughout the Middle East. Goat is also eaten by the Bedouin, and I once came upon a wedding in Abu Dhabi when a young camel had been slain and was cooking in an enormous pot of stew.

The roast stuffed lamb makes a nice Sunday lunch. You can use either a leg or a shoulder for this lamb, yoghurt and lemon recipe or *kharouf bi limoun* as it is known in Arabic. I have cooked this time and time again with unfailingly excellent results. Easily prepared, it is also a good choice if expecting guests on a week night. I serve it with boiled new potatoes liberally sprinkled with cumin, and either cold bean salad or a crisp green salad.

Of the other recipes, the okra stew recipe comes from Jordan; lamb and chick pea casserole is found throughout the Middle East (especially in Egypt when people can afford the meat); Syrian meatloaf is a useful dish – eat it hot first, then serve it cold with a salad; and I often cook *Lady's Thighs* to serve as starters at a cocktail party. They can be made before the guests arrive and kept warm in the oven.

Persian Casserole with Prunes

Serves about 6:
24 prunes
1.5 kg (3 lb) veal, cut into cubes
salt and pepper to taste
1 teaspoon ground cumin
juice of 3 lemons
120 ml (4 fl oz) cooking oil
3 tablespoons flaked almonds
50 g (2 oz) butter
2 medium onions, chopped
1 litre (1 3/4 pints) stock
1 1/2 tablespoons icing sugar

Soak the prunes overnight. Marinate the meat together with the seasonings in half the lemon juice and the oil. Leave for 2 hours. While the meat is marinating, brown the almonds on baking sheet and set aside.

Melt the butter in a deep frying pan and sauté the onion until soft. Drain the meat, add it to the frying pan and brown on all sides. Add the stock, cover the frying pan and simmer on a low heat for about 1 1/2 hours, or until tender. To reduce the amount of stock, cook uncovered for the final 30 minutes.

Drain the prunes, keeping 300 ml (1/2 pint) juice. Mix the icing sugar with juice and transfer to a large pan. Simmer gently for 15 minutes. Meanwhile stone the prunes.

When the meat is cooked, remove the pan from the heat, add the prunes, the prune juice, half the almonds and the rest of the lemon juice. Stir this in, and cook rapidly for 5 minutes. Remove from the heat and sprinkle with the remaining almonds. Serve with *chelo* rice (see page 76) and a green salad.

Roast Stuffed Neck of Lamb

Serves 4-6:

*1-1.5 kg (2-3 lb) boned neck of
  lamb*
juice of 2 medium onions
1 tablespoon ground coriander
1 teaspoon ground ginger
*salt and freshly ground black
  pepper*
2 tablespoons oil

Stuffing

225 g (8 oz) rice
*saffron to colour, or 1/2 teaspoon
  turmeric*
2 onions, chopped
*25 g (1 oz) pine nuts (or blanched
  almonds)*
1/2 teaspoon ground allspice
50 g (2 oz) butter
75 g (3 oz) sultanas
salt and black pepper

Wipe the inside and outside of the neck
with a cloth, rub well with onion juice and
seasonings and set aside.

To prepare the stuffing, cook the rice
until it is light and fluffy. Sauté the
onions, pine nuts and allspice in the butter,
then mix with the rice. Add the sultanas, mix
well and season with salt and pepper. Leave to
cool.

Preheat the oven to 220°C/425°F/Gas Mark
7. Spoon the stuffing on to the lamb and roll
up. Tie with cotton string. Rub with 1
tablespoon oil and sear in remaining oil in
oven.

Cook for 15 minutes, turning on all
sides, then reduce the heat to moderate
(190°C/375°F/Gas Mark 5). Roast at this heat,
turn once again, then allow to become crisp.
As for other lamb dishes, cooking time will
depend on how you like your meat. Allow
about 30 minutes per 225 g (1/2 pound).

Shoulder of Lamb with Saffron

Serves 4:

3 garlic cloves, peeled
1.25 kg (2 ½ lb) shoulder of lamb
1 teaspoon mixed herbs
salt and pepper
6 tablespoons olive oil
2 onions, sliced
juice of 2 lemons
pinch of cayenne pepper
saffron, to colour

Chop the garlic into slivers and insert in small cuts all over the lamb. Mix the herbs, salt, pepper and half the oil and marinate the lamb for 2 hours.

In a deep large frying pan, sauté the onion in the remaining oil until golden brown, then add the juice of 1 lemon, season with cayenne pepper, and simmer for 5 minutes. Remove to a large casserole. Preheat the oven to 180°C/350°F/Gas Mark 4.

Now heat the marinating oil in the frying pan, add the shoulder and sear on all sides. Add the juice of the second lemon mixed with the saffron and transfer to the casserole. Cook until tender, about 1 ½–2 hours.

Serve the lamb, carved into slices, garnished with sliced lemon and accompanied by rice.

Roast Leg of Lamb with Yoghurt and Lemon

Serves 6-8:

1 leg of lamb, about
1.75 kg (4 lb)
salt and freshly ground black
pepper
4 cloves garlic
6 tablespoons olive oil
6 tablespoons lemon juice, plus a
little grated lemon rind
150 ml (5 fl oz) natural yoghurt

Season the lamb well with salt and black pepper. Cut the garlic into small slivers and insert in cuts all over the leg. Set aside for 4 hours. Preheat the oven to 230°C/450°F/Gas Mark 8.

Heat the oil in a roasting dish in the oven until it sizzles, and sear the lamb on all sides, about 15 minutes. Remove from the oven and allow to cool slightly, then pour over half the lemon juice, the rind and half the yoghurt. Reduce the oven heat to about 190°C/375°F/

Gas Mark 5.

Replace the lamb in the oven and bake, turning once and adding more lemon juice and yoghurt. Add water if the lemon juice dries up. Do not turn after the final hour, to allow the yoghurt to form a golden brown crust.

Serve this crusty tender lamb in slices, with boiled new potatoes and cumin, and any of the green or tomato salads.

Okra and Lamb Stew

Serves 4-5:

750 g (1 ½ lb) young okra
vinegar
3 cloves garlic, crushed
1 teaspoon ground coriander
1 ½ tablespoons butter
1 kg (2 lb) lean lamb, cubed
6 medium ripe tomatoes (or
    275 g (10 oz) can with juice),
    chopped
350 ml (12 fl oz) meat stock
salt and freshly ground black
    pepper
1 ½ tablespoons lemon juice

Wash the okra and cut off the stems, taking care not to puncture the pods. Soak pods in vinegar for 30 minutes, then drain and dry on a kitchen paper.

Sauté the garlic and coriander in the butter in a large saucepan or casserole dish, then add the lamb and seal over a high heat. Turn each piece until it changes colour, then add the okra and tomatoes. Simmer for 5–10 minutes, then cover with the stock. Season with salt and pepper, stir well, and simmer on a low heat for 1 ½–2 hours, or until tender. By this time the sauce should be greatly reduced. Add the lemon juice just before serving.

Okra stew is a favourite in Jordan. Okra and lentils are two of the most common stew ingredients in the Middle East.

Lamb and Chick Pea Casserole

Serves 4-5:
450 g (1 lb) dried chick peas
600 ml (1 pint) water
1 large onion, chopped
4 cloves garlic, finely chopped
1 teaspoon ground allspice
1 teaspoon paprika
pinch of ground cumin
*salt and freshly ground black
    pepper*
*1.5 kg (3 lb) boned lamb cut into
    pieces*
*1 shin bone with marrow,
    chopped in 2-3 pieces*
450 g (1 lb) small aubergines
5 tablespoons olive oil
1 1/2 tablespoons lemon juice
*6 tablespoons tahini (sesame seed
    paste)*

Soak the chick peas overnight in cold water, then drain.

Put the water in a deep heavy casserole. Add the onion, garlic, chick peas and seasonings. Trim the lamb well, add to the casserole, cover with the marrowbones and simmer for about 2 hours.

When the meat is tender, remove from the heat and allow to cool. Extract the marrow and discard the large bones. Chill the dish while preparing the aubergines.

Soak the aubergines for 30 minutes in cold, salted water, then drain well, pat dry and slice thinly. Heat the olive oil in a frying pan and fry each piece a golden brown. Drain on kitchen paper and keep warm.

Remove the casserole from the refrigerator and skim the fat off the surface. Add more salt if necessary, plus a liberal amount of black pepper, and reheat in the oven. Now blend the lemon juice and *tahini* and add to the casserole. Stir in and simmer gently for 10 minutes. Transfer the casserole to a serving dish, add the aubergines and keep in the oven until ready to serve – about 10 minutes.

Serve with pita bread to mop up the rich sauce, and a chopped salad.

*Lamb and chick pea casserole
topped with sliced aubergine.
A substantial meal on a cold
night.*

Braised Chops with Vegetables

Serves 4:
courgettes, leeks (or other
*   vegetables), see recipe*
8-10 fleshy lamb chops
1 ½ tablespoons butter
1 large onion, sliced
2-3 cloves garlic, chopped
generous pinch of
*   coriander, paprika and*
*   ground allspice*
6 medium ripe tomatoes,
*   sliced*
2 tablespoons finely chopped
*   parsley*
salt and freshly ground black
*   pepper*
175 ml (6 fl oz) stock

Braised chops with vegetables
is widely eaten, especially in
rural areas.

Use 2 large courgettes or about 450 g (1 lb) leeks.

Trim the chops of any excess fat and brown in butter on both sides. Remove from the frying pan and place in a greased ovenproof dish. Preheat the oven to 190°C/375°F/Gas Mark 5.

Sauté the onion, garlic and spices in the butter remaining in the frying pan until softened. Add the tomatoes, half the parsley and the salt and pepper. Simmer for 10 minutes, then add the stock, mixing thoroughly.

Place the sliced vegetables on top of the chops, and pour the sauce mixture over them. Add more seasoning, as desired. Cook in the oven until the chops are tender and the sauce is rich and aromatic. Garnish with the remaining parsley. Serve with potato purée, or with baked potatoes, slashed open and garnished with butter and cumin.

Meatballs in Yoghurt Sauce

Serves 4:
1 kg (2 lb) lean minced beef
75 g (3 oz) bulghur (cracked
   wheat), soaked and dried
pinch each paprika and
   ground allspice
salt and freshly ground pepper
3 medium onions, very finely
   chopped
50 g (2 oz) pine nuts
1 1/2 tablespoons butter
cooking oil

Yoghurt sauce
200 ml (1/3 pint) natural yoghurt
1 tablespoon cornflour
salt and pepper, to taste
2-3 cloves garlic, crushed
2 tablespoons dried mint, crushed
butter, for frying

*Meatballs with yoghurt sauce
is served by most Syrian and
Lebanese restaurants. It is
eaten with rice and a salad.*

Mix together the meat, *bulghur* and spices as per the instructions for *kibbeh nayé* on page 35. Meanwhile sauté the onions and pine nuts lightly in the butter and allow to cool.

Break off lumps of meat the size of a golf ball and stuff with the pine nut and onion mixture. Heat the oil in a deep saucepan and fry the meatballs until crisp on the outside, but juicy within. Drain on a paper towel and keep warm.

To stabilise the yoghurt, pour it into a large saucepan and beat until liquid. Mix the cornflour with a little water to make a paste. Add this to the yoghurt together with a pinch of salt. Heat to just below boiling while stirring continuously in one direction. Continue to stir the mixture over a minimum heat, or until the sauce thickens. Do not cover, or overheat.

Sauté the garlic in a little butter, add the mint and mix this into the yoghurt sauce. Season further according to taste.

Place the meatballs in a serving dish and cover with the sauce. Serve with plain rice and chopped Arab salad, with bread to mop up the sauce.

Syrian Stuffed Kibbeh

Serves 4:
kibbeh recipe (page 35),
    using 75g (3 oz) bulghur
oil, for frying

Filling
1 medium onion, finely diced
25 g (1 oz) pine nuts
about 50 g (2 oz) butter
225 g (8 oz) finely minced lamb
½ teaspoon ground allspice
salt and freshly ground
    black pepper

Make the *kibbeh* mixture first.

To make the filling, sauté the onion and pine nuts in the butter. When they turn golden brown, add the meat and allspice to the pan, cooking lightly until the meat changes colour. Add salt and pepper and mix well. While this cools, prepare the *kibbeh* shells.

The Syrians are masters at making kibbeh, the pounding of the mince and bulghur being a familiar sound. Pictured on the right is stuffed kibbeh served with hummus and muhammara dips.

Break off a lump the size of a small egg, and cupping it in your palm, make a hole in the centre with your finger. Mould the paste around your finger, working up and down and round and round (a practice likened by Middle Eastern cookery expert, Claudia Roden, to pottery making). It is a difficult art: if the paste breaks, use moistened hands to stick it together again.

Now fill each egg shaped *kibbeh* with a little

stuffing. Seal the edges by wetting with iced water. As each *kibbeh* is made, set it aside on a tray (you can prepare them in advance and chill them).

Heat a deep frying pan with enough oil to cover the *kibbeh*. When the oil is sizzling, drop them in and cook on a high heat, turning frequently until they turn rich brown but the filling remains juicy. Drain on kitchen paper and serve either hot or cold, with a selection of dips and salads.

Ground Meat Kebabs

Serves 6:

1 kg (2 lb) lean minced beef or
     lamb
3 medium onions, finely
     chopped
6 tablespoons coarsely chopped
     parsley
salt and freshly ground black
     pepper
1/2 teaspoon ground allspice
1/2 teaspoon cayenne pepper
flour, for dusting
oil, for brushing

Light the barbecue (if using).
Put the meat into a food processor and work briefly until combined.

With moistened hands, break off walnut-sized lumps of the mixture and mould into sausage shapes around a skewer (two per skewer). You should fill 6 skewers in all. Dust with flour to hold firmly, then brush lightly with oil and cook over the barbecue or under a preheated grill, turning frequently.

Serve on a platter lined with lettuce, garnished with lemon wedges and *hummus* or *muhammara* side dips (see pages 24 and 28). Serve with rice and salad.

*Serve minced meat kebabs
with a dip like
hummus or muhammara or
babagannouj.*

Turkish-style Kebabs

The sizzle of grilling kebabs is music to the ears. Turkish-style kebabs.

Allow 450 g (8 oz) meat per person, to make 2 skewers each. Choose a lean piece of lamb or beef – and cut it into chunky cubes. Rub with salt and freshly ground black pepper and marinate in lemon juice, olive oil and marjoram for about 2 hours. (To make the *kebabs* more piquant, add a good pinch of paprika to the marinade.)

Cut up chunks of green or red pepper, onions and firm tomatoes to intersperse with the meat. Cored and halved kidneys are also delicious.

Impale the meat, onions, tomato and chunks of pepper alternately on the skewers and cook under a preheated grill, turning frequently until cooked on all sides.

Serve on the skewers with plain rice. Side dips are *hummus, muhammara* and *labneh*.

Syrian Meatloaf

Serves about 6-8:

25 g (1 oz) pine nuts
butter
2 eggs
2 medium onions, finely
*   chopped*
5 cm (2 inch) piece of fresh ginger,
*   grated*
3 tablespoons tomato purée
1 teaspoon ground allspice
salt and freshly ground black
*   pepper*
1 kg (2 lb) lean minced lamb
25 g (1 oz) fresh breadcrumbs
lemon wedges, cress or
*   parsley, to garnish*

First sauté the pine nuts lightly in a little butter and set aside. Heat the oven to 140°C/ 375°F/Gas Mark 5.

In a mixing bowl beat the eggs, then add the onions, purée, allspice, salt and pepper. Mix well.

Knead the lamb thoroughly in a mixing bowl. Make a hollow in the centre, pour in the egg mixture, add the pine nuts and mix well. Finally add the fresh breadcrumbs to bind the mixture. Form into a loaf shape, and sprinkle with a little cold water and dot with butter. Wrap in foil and bake for 1-1½ hours, unwrapping the foil for the final 30 minutes to allow to brown.

Syrian meatloaf may be served either hot or cold. This recipe leaves enough over to use cold; it is a good picnic dish. Serve with side dishes of *labneh* and salad.

Syrian meatloaf can be eaten hot or cold. Serve with a labneh dip and a lettuce salad.

Kidneys in Tomato Sauce

Serves 4:

12 lambs' kidneys
lemon juice or vinegar
2 onions, finely chopped
2 cloves garlic, crushed
pinch each of chilli powder,
    ground coriander,
    cumin, and chopped
    parsley
1 1/2 tablespoons butter
4 medium tomatoes, skinned
    and pulped
1 tablespoon tomato purée
salt and freshly ground black
    pepper

Soak the kidneys in water with 2 teaspoons of lemon juice or vinegar for about 2 hours. Drain, skin, slice in half and remove the cores. Cut into quarters.

Sauté the onion, garlic and seasonings in the butter. Add the kidneys and toss lightly until they change colour. Add the tomato pulp and purée, mixing well. Finally add the salt and pepper and 1–2 tablespoons water.

Cook gently on a low heat, about 10–15 minutes, according to how you like kidneys done. Serve with plain rice and a green salad.

Kidneys in tomato sauce. Offal is widely enjoyed throughout the Middle East. Yemenis eat liver and kidneys for breakfast.

Poultry Dishes

One medieval Middle Eastern recipe book lists over 300 different ways of cooking poultry, especially chicken. Apparently Kaskari chickens (Kaskar is a village between the Tigris and the Euphrates) were considered to have the best taste and, according to one translator, they grew "as heavy as a goat, or a sheep". The breeding of chickens appears to have been common at this time, yet it was not so long ago, especially in the Arab countries, that chickens were so scarce they were considered a luxury.

I recall an incident during travels through North Yemen when, invited to eat at a rural dwelling, I was sitting talking to my host. A terrible squawking came from below and peering out a window, I saw a boy chasing a scraggy hen until, with a well aimed stick, he

Chickens are in for a rough ride in North Yemen. More than 300 different ways of cooking poultry exist in the Middle East.

killed it. The fact that it was his father's only chicken underlined the family's incredible hospitality. Now ironically, like most Middle Eastern towns, Sana'a has a "Kentucky Fried Chicken" restaurant (although it was closed for months as the owner was rumoured to be a Jew!)

It is probably true that there are more ways of cooking poultry than any other ingredient in the Middle Eastern repertoire. Recipes in this chapter range from chicken *kebab* (cover illustration) to the exotic duckling in walnut and pomegranate sauce. Finding we were only two one Christmas, I cooked Persian chicken (stuffed with apricots, prunes, raisins and pine nuts) which was as good as, and much more economical than, the traditional English turkey.

There is a delicious recipe for lemon chicken (although it makes a mess of the grillpan). I serve it hot with a green side salad, but it is equally good cold. I once made it my basic dish for a picnic to watch the Oxford and Cambridge boat race: it poured with rain and the Cambridge crew sank – but the lemon chicken saved the day!

The recipe for chicken casseroled with lemon juice was supplied by the Holiday Inn in Amman. Easy to prepare, it can be made in advance for a dinner party.

Ferakh al-hara (hot chicken) is one of the easiest dishes to make in the book, an ideal recipe should you be eating alone after a busy day at work. I have a very "seasoned" palate, liking things hot, and tend to substitute chilli powder for the sweeter paprika.

Cafés in Amman and Jerusalem are famous for chicken *musakhan*, a take–out snack like *döner kebap*, or *shawarma* as it is known in Arabic. *Sumaka*, a red spice with a lemony tang gives it its characterisic flavour, but this is hard to buy in Britain.

As well as being masters at cooking chickens in so many different ways, Middle Eastern cooks take great pains to ensure that each dish has special eye appeal. Beautifully garnished with red paprika in oil and chopped walnuts, Circassian chicken is a good example. Side dishes are fluffy white rice and an emerald green salad.

Fesanjan, or tender duckling steeped in walnuts and pomegranates, is the king of all the poultry dishes. The medieval Persian recipe conjures up all the pomp and pageantry of the glorious reign of the Safavid *shahs*. If you can't find fresh pomegranates, use lemon juice or pomegranate juice concentrate, but the appearance of the dish will obviously suffer.

Restaurants in Lebanon have traditionally served small birds as *mezze*. Rubbed with salt, pepper and olive oil, they are grilled on skewers over a charcoal fire. A restaurant in the mountain town of Bhamdoun was famous for birds served in this manner. In Egypt, migrating quail are netted near Agami, a popular beach resort with Cairo's élite near Alexandria. Syrian farmers, especially around Aleppo, breed pigeons for the family pot.

Lemon Chicken Casserole

Serves 4-5:
1 x 1.5 kg (3 lbs) chicken or
  2 small chickens
3 medium onions, chopped
3 cloves garlic, crushed
about 6 tablespoons lemon
  juice
salt and pepper
1 1/2–2 tablespoons butter
pinch of paprika
parsley, to garnish

Skin and bone the chickens and cut the flesh into cubes. Mix these with the onions, garlic, lemon juice, salt and pepper in a large bowl. Cover, chill and marinate for 12 hours.

In a deep saucepan, sauté the chicken mixture in the butter, then add 1 cup of half water and lemon juice to taste. Cover and simmer on a low heat until tender, about 20 minutes. Serve with saffron rice, garnished with paprika and parsley.

Lemon chicken casserole is easy to prepare. A good recipe for weight watchers.

Chicken in Yoghurt

Serves 4:
110 oz (4 oz) butter
1 x 1.25–1.5 kg (2 1/2–3 lb) chicken,
* cut into 8 pieces*
4 shallots, finely chopped
small bunch of parsley,
* chopped*
1 teaspoon dried thyme
300 ml (1/2 pint) chicken stock
1/2 teaspoon salt
freshly ground black pepper
juice of 1 lemon
2 teaspoons plain flour
120 ml (4 fl oz) single cream
65 ml (2 1/2 fl oz) natural yoghurt

Melt the butter in a large deep frying pan. Add the chicken pieces and cook, turning frequently, until golden brown on all sides, about 10–15 minutes. Add shallots, the parsley and thyme and cook until the shallots are transparent.

Add the stock, salt and lots of pepper, and simmer on a low heat for 30 minutes, turning the chicken pieces at intervals. If the sauce evaporates too quickly add a little of the lemon juice and some water. Meanwhile preheat the oven to 230°C/450°F/Gas Mark 8. Mix the flour with the cream, blend in the yoghurt and add the lemon juice.

Now grease a shallow ovenproof dish and place the chicken in it. Pour the sauce from the skillet into the cream mixture and blend slowly. Pour this mixture over the chicken and cook for 15 minutes. Reduce the heat to 180°C/350°F/Gas Mark 4, and cook for a further 15 minutes. Serve with puréed potatoes and a green salad.

Chicken in yoghurt sauce is an Egyptian favourite. Dip Arab bread in the sauce.

Ferakh al-hara *Hot Chicken*

Serves 4:
5 tablespoons olive oil
juice of 1 lemon
1 teaspoon chilli powder,
   to taste
salt and pepper
1 heaped teaspoon crushed
   garlic
1 x 1 kg (2 lb) chicken,
   cut into 4 pieces
lemon wedges, to garnish

Preheat the oven to 190°C/375°F/Gas Mark 5.
Mix the oil, lemon juice, chilli, salt, pepper
and garlic in a bowl.
   Place the chicken pieces in a baking dish
and cover with the mixture. Bake for 15–20
minutes, basting occasionally. Do not baste
for the final 15–20 minutes to allow the
chicken to become crisp.
   Serve with a rice *pilaf* and salad or as
desired. Garnish with lemon wedges.

Ferakh al-hara or "hot chicken" can be made as hot as you want. Serve with plain rice and a green salad

Chicken Musakhan

Serves 6:

1 x 1.5 kg (3 lb) chicken, cut into 6 portions
450 ml (3/4 pint) chicken stock
1 small celery, stalk with leaves
1 medium onion, sliced
salt and pepper
4 small onions sliced into fine rings
1 tablespoon pine nuts
3 tablespoons oil
6 pita breads
2 teaspoons sumak (if available)

Place the chicken stock pieces in a casserole, cover with the stock and add the celery, the sliced onion and salt and pepper. Cover and simmer until tender, about 40 minutes. Remove the chicken and set aside a little of the stock. While the chicken is cooking, sauté the onion rings and pine nuts in the oil.

Arrange the bread on the grill tray and top each piece with a portion of chicken, some of the onion rings and dribble a little stock over them. Sprinkle each with *sumak* and grill until the chicken turns golden brown. Take care not to burn the bread. Serve garnished with pine nuts and extra onion rings.

Musakhan can be eaten by itself, or with a salad. It is a novel ideal for lunch in the garden.

Chicken musakhan is a popular snack at cafés in Amman. It is sprinkled with sumak, a lemon-tasting spice.

Persian Chicken

Serves 6:
2 medium onions, finely
  chopped
100 g (4 oz) butter
40 g (1½ oz) raisins
175 g (6 oz) dried prunes, soaked,
  stoned and sliced
175 g (6 oz) dried apricots, soaked
  and sliced
1 teaspoon ground cinnamon
salt and freshly ground black
  pepper
1 x 1.75 kg (4 lb) chicken

Sauté the onion in half the butter for a few minutes, then add the fruits and sauté gently for a further 5 minutes. Season the mixture with cinnamon, salt and pepper, and allow to cool.

Heat the oven to 190°C/375°F/Gas Mark 5. Stuff the chicken with the fruit mixture. Sew the neck flap to keep the moisture in. Rub all over with salt, pepper and remaining butter, wrap in foil and bake in the oven.

Open the foil after 40 minutes so the skin will brown and become crisp. The cooking time is approximately 1½–2 hours.

Stuffed with dried fruits, Persian chicken makes an unusual dish for a small dinner party.

Circassian Chicken

Serves 4-5:
1 x 1.5 kg (3 lb) chicken
1 large onion, chopped
1 clove garlic, chopped
2 celery sticks, chopped
salt and freshly ground black
*   pepper*
350 g (12 oz) long-grain rice
90 g (3 ½ oz) walnuts, finely
*   chopped*
2 tablespoons olive oil
1 teaspoon paprika

Put the chicken, onion, garlic, celery, salt and pepper in a large saucepan, cover with water and simmer until tender, about 1½ hours. Remove and drain the chicken (reserving the stock), and keep warm in a low oven.

Chill the stock quickly, then skim as much fat as possible off the surface.

Cook the rice (see pages 76–7), and keep warm in a low oven.

Meanwhile make the sauce. Put the ground walnuts in a deep frying pan and add 300 ml (10 fl oz) of stock. Bring to the boil, then simmer on a high heat, stirring until the mixture thickens. Season with more salt and pepper.

Now blend the oil and the paprika until the oil becomes bright red. Cut the chicken into attractive serving portions, arrange them on a bed of the rice. Cover with the sauce and trickle the red oil on top.

Circassian chicken makes an attractive presentation. Yoghurt and water is a common beverage in the Middle East. Also pictured are tomato and coriander salad and plain rice.

Roast Chicken stuffed with Rice and Pine Nuts

Serves 6:

1 large onion, finely chopped
100 g (4 oz) butter, melted
75 g (3 oz) chicken livers,
*   minced*
225 g (8 oz) sausagemeat
175 g (6 oz) long-grain rice
50 g (2 oz) pine nuts
1/2 teaspoon ground cinnamon
1/4 teaspoon ground allspice
salt and freshly ground black
*   pepper*
1 cup of chicken stock
1 x 1.75 kg (4 lb) chicken

Using a deep frying pan sauté the onion in two-thirds of the melted butter until it turns soft and golden. Add the liver and sausagemeat and toss until lightly brown. Next add the rice, pine nuts, cinnamon, allspice, salt and pepper and cook about 5 minutes. To this add the stock and cook over a low heat until it is absorbed, about 12–15 minutes. Allow to cool. Preheat the oven to 190°C/375°F/Gas Mark 5.

Rub the entire chicken with salt and pepper. Spoon in the stuffing and close the openings with either small skewers or thread.

Brush with remaining melted butter and roast until the chicken is crisp and tender, about 2 hours. To crisp the skin, do not baste for the last 30 minutes.

Roast chicken with pine nut stuffing will impress dinner guests.

Chicken Kebabs *(Cover illustration)*

Serves 3-4:

1 x 1.25 kg (2³/4 lb) chicken,
*   boned and cut into good*
*   sized cubes (see recipe)*
6 tablespoons olive oil
6 tablespoons lemon juice
2 cloves garlic, crushed
salt and freshly ground black
*   pepper*
1 tablespoon melted butter
saffron to colour, or ¹/2 teaspoon
*   turmeric*

A barbecue is ideal for cooking these chicken *kebabs,* but a good grill is perfectly adequate. The chicken pieces should be of a size that will stay firmly on the skewers (leaving the skin on helps). Combine the oil, lemon juice, garlic, salt and pepper in a bowl, and place the chicken cubes in it. Cover and marinate for several hours, turning occasionally. Preheat the grill or light the barbecue.

Dissolve the saffron or turmeric in the melted butter. Thread the chicken pieces on skewers and brush with this mixture. Cook over or under a high heat, turning and basting frequently with the butter, for about 15 minutes.

Serve the *kebabs* on the skewers on a bed of saffron rice (see page 76) garnished with sliced oranges. A plain lettuce salad would complement the meal nicely.

Chicken kebab (cover illustration).
Middle Eastern cooks pay
great attention to visual appeal.

Grilled Lemon Chicken

Serves 6:
*1 large onion, very finely
  chopped
juice of 2 large lemons
5 tablespoons peanut butter
175 ml (6 fl oz) olive oil
salt, to taste
freshly ground black pepper
2 x 1 kg (2 lb) chickens, each cut
  into 6 pieces*

Mix the onion, lemon juice, peanut butter,
oil, salt and pepper well and brush on the
chicken pieces. Place under a medium–hot
grill and cook until tender. Turn the
pieces and baste frequently with the
mixture, watching that it does not burn.
Serve when golden brown and tender.

The chicken pieces may be eaten hot, or
cold, with a lettuce salad and rice *pilaf.*

*Peanut butter forms a
delicious crust on lemon
chicken. Excellent hot or cold.
An ideal picnic dish.*

Chicken with Olives

Serves 4:
1 chicken, about 1.5 kg (3 lb),
* cut into 8 pieces*
350 g (12 oz) green olives,
* stoned and chopped*
salt and pepper
3 cloves garlic, crushed
2 tablespoons olive oil
1 teaspoon grated fresh
* ginger root*
1 teaspoon turmeric, or 2-3
* strands of saffron*
350 ml (12 fl oz) chicken stock
1 teaspoon paprika
1 teaspoon ground cumin
6 tablespoons lemon juice

Bring the chopped olives to the boil 3 times in a deep saucepan. Change the water each time, the last time using 300 ml (½ pint) water with a pinch of salt. Remove from the stove and press the olives down with a potato masher to extract more juices. Set aside.

Sauté the garlic in the oil in a large, deep frying pan. Add the ginger, turmeric or saffron, the chicken pieces and the stock. Cover and cook slowly on a medium heat, turning at intervals, about 30–40 minutes.

When the chicken is tender, remove it from the pan and keep warm. Now reduce the broth until it becomes thick and pungent. Add the paprika, cumin, lemon juice and more salt and pepper according to taste. Simmer for a minute, then add the olives and their juices, stir well and allow the sauce to further thicken, about 12-15 minutes.

When ready to serve, return the chicken portions to the pan and heat in the sauce. Serve each portion garnished with olives, with pita bread to mop up the sauce, rice *pilaf* and chopped salad.

Braised chicken with olives.
Serve with rice pilaf and bread
to mop up the rich sauce.

Duck in Walnut and Pomegranate Sauce

Serves 4:
1 duck, about 1.75 kg (4 lb)
salt and freshly ground black
  pepper
1 ¹/₂ tablespoons clarified butter
2 medium onions, chopped
150 g (5 oz) brown sugar
1 teaspoon ground cinnamon
9 tablespoons pomegranate juice
  (about 3 fruits) or use
  grenadine syrup
450 ml (15 fl oz) homemade stock
100 g (4 oz) chopped walnuts

Garnish *(optional)*
100 g (4 oz) chopped walnuts
seeds of 2 pomegranates

Rub the duck well with salt and pepper.
Melt the butter in a deep frying pan and
brown the duck on all sides. Remove and
keep warm in a low oven.

Drain the excess fat from the pan and sauté
the onion until soft and transparent. Add the
sugar, cinnamon, pomegranate juice and
stock, stir well and simmer uncovered for
about 12 minutes.

Remove the duck from the oven and
increase the temperature to 220°C/425°F/Gas
Mark 7. Melt some butter in a roasting tin,
add the duck and put in the oven. After 10
minutes, drain off excess fat and reduce the
oven to 190°C/375°F/Gas Mark 5.

Now spoon half the pomegranate sauce
over the duck and continue to baste
frequently except for the final 30 minutes of
cooking. Turn only once during this time,
after about 1½ hours. Drain the fat as it

separates from the sauce.

When the duck is nearly cooked, add the
chopped walnuts to the remaining sauce in
the pan, adjust the seasoning as necessary, stir
well, simmer on a low heat for 5–10 minutes,
and keep warm.

Continue to drain excess fat off the duck,
being careful not to waste any of the sauce.
The skin should turn a crisp, rosy brown.

There are two options when serving
fesanjan. For eye appeal, present the duck
whole, garnished with the sauce, the
chopped walnuts and pomegranate seeds.
Alternatively carve it, and pour the sauce
over each serving. You can also leave the
sauce for people to help themselves. Serve
with *chelo* (see page 76) and a lettuce salad.

Seafood

Buying the family fish in Bahrain. The Arabian Gulf is renowned for excellent seafood.

Some of my most memorable meals in the Middle East have been seafood – but then I love fish. The setting of many seafood restaurants is also a bonus. How could I forget grilled fish by the creaking water wheels on the Orontes river at Hama, in Syria?

There is a restaurant near the Roman city of Jerash, in Jordan, which serves wonderful grilled perch – known locally as St Peter's fish – from the Sea of Galilee. More rustic is a restaurant in Aqaba with *al fresco* tables under half a dozen straggly palms. The fish is good – you choose your own in the kitchen – but the smell of the charcoal grill attracts Aqaba's 100,000 cats who practically drag it off your table.

Baghdad is famous for open-air restaurants serving *mashgouf* or smoked fish along the banks of the Tigris. The Iraqis do interesting things with fish, especially in the delta port of Basra, but some of the best seafood dishes are found in the Arabian Gulf. Despite oil spillages, the tepid waters of the Gulf abound in seafood: fish, crab, giant prawns and a delicately flavoured, flat-chested cousin of the lobster known as *Umm Robien*.

Hotels have a field day with such a variety of fish. No one chooses smoked Scottish salmon from the Bahrain Hilton buffet, but the local prawns, crayfish and cold cod disappear in minutes.

The early morning fish markets of Manama, capital of Bahrain, Kuwait, Dubai and the other Gulf states are a hive of activity the moment the *dhows* unload. In Muscat, capital of the

Sultanate of Oman, sardines and other fish are sold straight from smaller boats known as *houris*.

The Red Sea off Yemen and Saudi Arabia is equally rich in fish: barracuda, bass, cod, lobster and crabs. While the *Quran* imposes no dietary restrictions, shellfish are avoided by many Muslims, a parallel with Judaic dietary laws which forbid eating any fish without fins or scales.

And while the Mediterranean lapping southern Europe grows daily more toxic, the Eastern Mediterranean and the Aegean supply Turkey, Syria and Lebanon with a veritable treasure trove of seafood. One of the many delights of Istanbul is lunch at a sunny seafood restaurant beneath the Galatea Bridge linking the European and Asian sides of the city. At night seafood restaurants along the Bosphorus are packed.

The world's finest caviar comes from the Caspian Sea in northern Iran. The sturgeon are netted as they congregate to spawn and the eggs are scooped from the living fish. During travels around the Caspian Sea, I ate beluga caviar daily for lunch, with a raw onion, lemon, salty butter and local bread. Then back in Tehran, I enjoyed beluga caviar with sour cream and *blinis*.

The most popular eating fish in the Middle East are red mullet (known by the grand title of *Sultan Ibrahim* in Arabic), *arous*, a fish like the French *daurade* or sea bream, sole, sea bass, tuna and turbot.

Among freshwater fish, the *chahoute* (similar to a trout) is netted in the Tigris-Euphrates river systems in Iraq. This is the famous *mashgouf* which is cleaned, split, staked and smoked around an open fire. Pungent and tender, it is impossible to copy in a kitchen. In Basra and the Arabian Gulf States, fish baked in date purée is popular.

Tuna and swordfish *kebabs* are a speciality of Turkey where coastal restaurants also serve stuffed mussels and squid. *Samak mashi* or stuffed fish, fish baked in *tahini* sauce and baked fish eaten with *muhammara* are common in Syria and Lebanon. Arabs eat basically the same fish dishes, although an Indian influence has made seafood curries equally popular. Nile fish tend to taste muddy, but there are good seafood restaurants in Suez and Alexandria, *saadiyeh*, or plain fish and rice, and grilled or fried small fish being common dishes.

Some Middle Eastern countries still enjoy traditional dried, salted fish. A common sight in Dhofar, in southern Oman, are sheets of silver sardines drying along the beaches.

Wasif, tiny fish like sprats, are salted and dried by fishermen on the Tihama coast of North Yemen. Trucked to the mountain towns, they are sold by the basketful in local *souqs*. The fish adds zest to *zahawiq*, a popular Yemeni dip made from tomatoes and chillis.

Essentials for cooking fish the Middle Eastern way are plenty of olive oil, lemon and cumin. Skewers are needed for *kebab*-style fish while a fish clamp is necessary for a large whole fish. It will prevent it from breaking when it is turned over on the barbecue or under the grill.

Cold Fish in Olive Oil

Serves 4:

1 x 1 kg (2 lb) whole fish (cod, bass, mackerel or similar), gutted
6 tablespoons olive oil
1 large green pepper, seeded and finely chopped
2 medium onions, sliced
3 cloves garlic, crushed
6 medium tomatoes, peeled and sliced or a 400 g (14 oz) can
1 tablespoon tomato purée
a bunch of parsley, finely chopped
salt and pepper
6 green and 6 black olives, to garnish

Wash the fish and scrape off any loose scales and pat dry on a kitchen paper. If the skin is thick, make several diagonal slits to aid cooking. Heat the oil in a large pan and fry the fish slowly, cooking lightly on both sides (about 10 minutes). Lift out gently, drain on kitchen paper and allow to cool.

Sauté the green pepper in the same oil, then add the onion after 5 minutes and cook until both are soft. Add the garlic and sauté for a further 2 minutes. Pulp the tomatoes and blend with the purée and parsley. Add to the pan, season to taste, stir well and simmer for 15 minutes.

Lift the fish carefully back into the pan, cover with the sauce and cook gently for 10–15 minutes. If the sauce is too thick, add a little water mixed with lemon juice.

Finally, remove the fish to a large serving dish and pour the sauce over it. Surround it with the olives, cool and then refrigerate. Remove about 10 minutes before eating.

Cold fish salad is ideal for a summer buffet table.

Dublin Bay Prawn Curry

This recipe is based on a popular dish made from *Umm Robien*, a type of lobster found in the Arabian Gulf. It can be adapted to shrimps, crayfish or other shellfish.

Serves 4:
6-8 Dublin Bay prawns
2 tablespoons olive oil
juice of 1 large lemon
salt and black pepper
3 medium onions, sliced
1 bay leaf
1 celery stalk
2 cloves garlic, crushed
1 1/2 tablespoons clarified butter
2.5 cm (1 inch) fresh root ginger, peeled and grated
1 level teaspoon turmeric
1 teaspoon ground coriander
1/2 teaspoon ground cumin
1/2 teaspoon chilli powder
1 heaped tablespoon shredded coconut
4 medium tomatoes, skinned and chopped
freshly chopped coriander, to garnish

First prepare the prawns: remove the shells and heads and marinate in olive oil and some of the lemon juice with seasoning for 2 hours. Put the shells in a pan, cover with cold water, add 3 slices onion, a bay leaf, celery stalk and salt and pepper. Simmer until you have a rich, aromatic stock. Strain well and set aside.

In a large saucepan, sauté the garlic and remaining onion in the clarified butter until soft and transparent. Add the spices and coconut and sizzle for 1 minute.

Now add the tomato and remaining lemon juice and cook for 10 minutes, stirring well. Stir in the stock, marinade and prawns, and simmer uncovered until the prawns are tender and the sauce is reduced, about 15–20 minutes.

Garnish with finely chopped coriander leaves and serve with rice *pilaf.*

Dublin Bay prawn curry from the United Arab Emirates has a hint of India. Use any long-tailed crustacean for this.

Fried Fish

Serves 4:

*8 small fish (fresh sardines or
    herrings)*
4 cloves garlic, finely chopped
1/2 teaspoon ground cumin
salt and white pepper
*1 1/2 tablespoons finely chopped
    parsley*
plain flour, to coat
cooking oil
*sliced lemon and tomato, to
    garnish*

Wash and clean the fish under running
water, then pat dry on kitchen paper.

Mix the garlic, cumin, salt and pepper
and parsley together and rub over the fish
inside and out. Cover and chill for 1 hour so
the fish will absorb the flavours.

Now roll each fish in the flour. Heat
enough oil in a frying pan to shallow fry
them. When it is sizzling hot, slip each fish in
and cook quickly on both sides, about 10
minutes. Serve garnished with lemon and
tomato.

Prawns in Tomato Sauce

Serves 4:

1 kg (2 lb) shelled prawns
1/2 teaspoon ground cinnamon
salt and freshly ground pepper
3 cloves garlic, crushed
2 medium onions, finely
*   chopped*
1 1/2 tablespoons oil
3 tablespoons tomato purée
5 medium ripe tomatoes,
*   peeled, chopped and puréed*
3 tablespoons lemon juice
freshly chopped parsley

Season the prawns with cinnamon, salt and pepper.

Sauté the garlic and onions in the oil until they are soft. Blend in the tomato purée diluted with a little water. Add this to the pan mixture and mix in the fresh tomato purée, stirring well. Allow to simmer on a gentle heat, about 12 minutes.

Add the prawns and cook on a medium to high heat for about 10 minutes. Stir frequently and remove from heat when tender. Sprinkle with lemon juice and parsley and serve on a bed of plain rice.

Prawns in tomato sauce. This recipe is from Saudi Arabia.

Baked Fish with Saffron Rice

Serves 4:

*1 large whole fish (sea bass
    or sea bream), 1.75 kg (4 lb),
    gutted*
3 cloves garlic, crushed
olive oil
fresh lemon juice
*salt and freshly ground black
    pepper*
1 large tomato, sliced
1 lemon, sliced
*1 quantity Saffron Rice (see
    page 76)*
lemon wedges and parsley

Wash and clean the fish under running water
and pat it dry with kitchen paper.
Rub over inside and out with a mixture of
garlic, oil, lemon juice, salt and pepper.
Place the tomato and lemon slices inside the
fish and sew up with cotton thread or skewer
closed. Chill for 2 hours. Heat oven to 190°C/
375°F/Gas Mark 5.
   Place the fish in a large, greased baking
dish and cook for 40–50 minutes until the flesh
is tender and the skin golden brown.
   Serve on a bed of saffron rice and
garnished with lemon wedges and parsley.

*Baked fish served on saffron
rice is the most common way
of presenting fish.*

Barbecued Fish with Dates

Serves 4:
225 g (8 oz) dried, stoned dates
4 whole white fish, about
    350 g (12 oz) each
salt and pepper
2 medium onions, finely
    chopped
1 clove garlic, crushed
1/2 teaspoon turmeric
generous pinch each of
    ground cumin, coriander,
    cardamon, nutmeg and
    cloves

Soak the dates in cold water until they become soft – about 4 hours. Gut and rinse the fish well under cold running water. Do not scale. Dry the cavities with kitchen paper and sprinkle with a little salt and pepper.

Mix the onion, garlic and spices with a little water and stuff each fish with this, sewing up the cavities, or securing with skewers.

Drain the dates then purée in a blender with a little water, or put through a sieve. Blend just long enough to obtain a soft paste, then smear this on both sides of each fish. Cook

over a barbecue, about 5 minutes each side. Test with a fork to make sure the flesh is tender. A fish clamp is useful for the dish.

Serve hot with a rice dish. The skin together with the scales can be peeled off when eating. The date purée gives the flesh a pleasant nutty flavour.

Fish in Hot Sauce

Serves 4:
4 cloves garlic, chopped
1 1/2 teaspoons ground
*   coriander*
4 thick fillets white fish, about
*   350 g (12 oz) each*
1 1/2 tablespoons olive oil
1 tablespoon lemon juice
salt and white pepper
lemon slices, to garnish

Sauce
50 g (2 oz) butter
1/2 small red pepper, diced
4 medium tomatoes, skinned
*   and chopped*
1 large onion, diced
1 teaspoon paprika
1/2 teaspoon ground ginger
pinch of salt and pepper
1 tablespoon tomato purée
*   mixed with a little water*

Pound the garlic and coriander together in a pestle and mortar. Rub this into the fish fillets and chill in a covered bowl for 2 hours.

Heat the oven to 190°C/375°F/Gas Mark 5. Remove the fish from the bowl and rub with a mixture of the oil, lemon juice, salt and pepper. Lay the fillets in a flat, oiled baking dish, cover tightly with foil and bake for about 20-30 minutes.

Meanwhile, prepare the sauce. Melt the butter in a pan and sauté the pepper, tomato and onion until soft. Add the seasonings and the tomato purée and mix well. Simmer for 10-15 minutes on a low heat.

Serve the fish in the baking dish, garnished with the hot sauce and lemon slices.

In the Levant, fish fillets or whole fish are baked and eaten with *muhammara* as a side dip. Some people even spread it over their fish.

Baked Fish in Tahini Sauce

Serves 4:
1 whole white fish, or 4
  fillets, about 1.25 kg (2½ lb)
  total weight
juice of 2 large lemons
salt and pepper
6 tablespoons olive oil
6 tablespoons tahini *(sesame*
  seed paste)
1 large onion, chopped
parsley, to garnish

Preheat oven to 200°C/400°F/Gas Mark 6.
Gut, scale and clean fish under running
water. Dry, and sprinkle with lemon juice.
Chill for 2 hours. Remove to room
temperature and rub with salt, pepper and
some of the oil. Bake for 20 minutes, or until

tender. While the fish cooks, sauté the onion
in the remaining oil.

Meanwhile blend the *tahini* and lemon
juice, adding water to achieve a creamy
sauce. Remove the fish from the oven,
sprinkle with the onions and coat with the
tahini sauce. Return to the oven and bake a
further 10 minutes. Garnish with parsley and
serve with rice and a salad.

Tuna Shashlik

Serves 4:
450 g (1 lb) fresh tuna
2 lemons
10 bay leaves
3 tablespoons olive oil
salt and black pepper
8 cherry tomatoes
bunch of fresh thyme
6 button onions

Skin and bone the tuna and cut into chunks. Put into a bowl with the juice of 1 lemon, the bay leaves and the oil. Grind black pepper over it, mix well and marinate for 1 hour, turning frequently.

Meanwhile wash the tomatoes. Make a small incision in the tops and squeeze out the seeds. Insert a drop of oil, salt, and a few thyme leaves in each.

Slice the second lemon. Thread the fish, the onions, tomatoes, bay leaves and lemon slices alternately on a skewer. Pour the remaining marinade over it and season with salt and pepper.

Cook under a preheated hot grill for about 10 minutes – then serve immediately with rice *pilaf* and a green salad.

Tuna shashlik is eaten with rice. Skewered fish is popular in the Eastern Mediterranean and in Egypt.

Stuffed Squid

Serves 4 *as a main course
with salads etc.,*
*6 medium squid (bodies about
    15 cm (6 inches long)*
5 tablespoons olive oil
*5 tablespoons thick tomato
    juice, or 2 medium tomatoes,
    skinned and pulped*
salt and pepper
pinch of paprika
juice of 1 lemon

Stuffing
*2 medium onions, finely
    chopped*
3 tablespoons olive oil
75 g (3 oz) rice
*1 tablespoon of dill or
    mint, finely chopped*
*2 tablespoons parsley, finely
    chopped*
1 tablespoon pine nuts
a pinch of ground cumin

To clean the squid, hold the body in one hand and gently pull off the head and arms: the innards and clear "quill" should come away as well. Clean the body thoroughly under cold running water, discarding anything left inside. Rub off any pigmentation from the body and set aside. Chop off the tentacles and put aside for the stuffing. Discard the heads.

In a glass bowl, mix the olive oil, the tomato juice, salt, pepper and paprika. Place the squid bodies in this mixture, coat well and leave to marinate while you make the stuffing.

In a large pan, sauté the onions in the oil until soft. Add the chopped tentacles and cook with the onion until they change colour. Now add the rice, dill or mint, parsley, pine nuts and cumin and cook 5–10 minutes, stirring with a wooden spoon. Leave to cool. Preheat the oven to 200°C/400°F/Gas 6.

Remove the squids from the marinade and partly fill each one with some of the stuffing. Allow room for the rice to swell during cooking. Secure the opening of each body with cocktail sticks, or thread.

Arrange the squid in a lightly oiled baking dish, cover with the marinade, the lemon juice and enough boiling water to almost cover them. Bake for about 50 minutes until tender. Remove and cool. Serve cold.

Stuffed squid are worth the preparation. Serve with a salad and bread to mop up any sauce. Tiny grilled squid are sometimes served in a mezze.

Desserts and Sweetmeats

The oldest known Islamic sweetmeat is *faludhaj*, a Persian concoction of ground almonds, sugar, rose water and other ingredients, which is believed to have been introduced in Mecca to cater for pilgrims making the *haj* or pilgrimage.

Ancient Arab and Farsi records make little reference to other rich desserts, but the Muslim sweet tooth can be traced back at least as far as the Abbasid caliphate. Recipe books from this period indicate that Abbasid society was addicted to sweetmeats, a taste not restricted to affluent families.

Among a variety of rich sweetmeats were *lawzinia* (a confection of almonds, breadcrumbs and syrup), *zalabiya* (an almond and rose water flavoured tart) and *khabis,* which seems to have been a gelatine-like dessert made with breadcrumbs, milk, sugar and sesame seed oil. Sugar, honey, molasses and syrup were commonly used sweeteners. Many people in the Middle East still believe that eating honey and other sweet things will ward off the "evil eye".

Sweets figure in many prominent dates in the Muslim calendar. Prior to *Muharram* (the first ten days of the New Year) or on the Prophet's birthday, housewives are busy cooking traditional sweetmeats. It is a custom to take these to relatives and friends who similarly call with their own homemade specialities.

Baklava is probably the best known sweetmeat. I have eaten *baklava* in places as far apart as Dakar and Sydney – wherever there are Lebanese, Turkish or

Baking biscuits in Baghdad, centre of Islam under the Abbasid caliphs. Many recipes originate from this period.

Armenian migrants. The Greeks also claim it is their own invention, but its true origins are obscure. *Baklava* keeps quite well, but it is best eaten within a day or two of preparation. It can be made using either walnuts or pistachio nuts.

Basbousa is another syrupy sweetmeat which can be made with yoghurt or coconut. It may be eaten hot or cold, with or without cream.

There can be few people who have never tasted *lokum*, or Turkish Delight as it is more commonly known. Many restaurants habitually offer a dish with coffee. I have not supplied a recipe for Turkish Delight as it can be readily bought and it is *so* time consuming to prepare. Also served with coffee are delicate almond fingers, a truly magical sweetmeat which I have enjoyed in many Middle Eastern homes.

Ma'moul are bite-sized pastries of many different shapes and fillings. Outside the great Ummayad Mosque in Damascus is a shop selling them oven-warm. You can buy a bag for under a pound to eat as you wander through the bazaar, one of the biggest and most interesting in the Middle East.

Dates have a myriad uses in Middle Eastern cookery. The Bedouin often eat them with bread and yoghurt as a substantial meal. They can be stuffed with marzipan or puréed to give a nutty flavour to fish. Tribes in remote parts of Saudi Arabia sustain their camels on date meal.

While the West Bank town of Jericho is more famous for citrus fruits, bananas also flourish in the almost semi-tropical climate of the Jordan Valley trench. Plantations can be seen on either side of the River Jordan and after the harvest, bananas hang side by side with oranges and grapefruit in Jericho's roadside stalls. Banana cake or banana loaf is an old Palestinian recipe, sometimes sold in shops, more often made at home.

Recipes appear for three glorious Middle Eastern desserts. My own favourite, *ma'mounia* or "Caliph's Delight", is a recipe said to have been created for the Caliph Ma'moun. A speciality of the Syrian town of Aleppo, it is often eaten for breakfast smothered in cream. Local folklore says it assists a woman to regain her strength after childbirth – what it does for men being something of a moot point. Similar to the drier *basbousa*, which is also made from farina, *ma'mounia* is extravagantly rich.

Made from ground rice, *muhallabia* is to the Middle East what rice pudding is to England or America. A very simple, delicately flavoured dish, it is eaten throughout the region, then under the name of *firni*, it pops up in Pakistan having probably been introduced by invading Mughals.

Umm Ali, or "Mother of Ali", is a very rich pudding, very fattening and utterly irresistible if you have a sweet tooth. Dried fruit salad can be made with many different combinations of dried fruits and nuts. It is served when Muslims break the fast at dusk. Eat it with cream and be sure to make enough to have on breakfast cereal – it's delicious.

"Caliph's Delight"

Serves 6:
450 ml (³/4 pint) water
juice of 1 lemon
225 g (8 oz) white sugar
100 g (4 oz) butter
25 g (1 oz) pine nuts
120 g (4¹/2 oz) semolina
300 ml (¹/2 pint) double cream
ground cinnamon, to sprinkle

Combine the water, lemon juice and sugar in a saucepan, bring to the boil and simmer for 15 minutes.

In a large frying pan, melt the butter and lightly sauté the pine nuts. Add the semolina and cook on a low heat until the semolina turns light brown, about 5 minutes.

Remove from the heat and stir in the syrup.

Return to a low heat, stir well and cook for a further 5 minutes. Transfer the mixture to a serving dish. Whip the cream lightly and smooth over the mixture. Sprinkle with cinnamon and serve.

Umm Ali *"Mother of Ali"*

Serves 6:
275 g (10 oz) cooked puff pastry
50 g (2 oz) pistachio nuts,
  chopped
50 g (2 oz) flaked almonds,
  toasted
1 1/2 tablespoons lemon juice
250 ml (8 fl oz) milk
175 g (6 oz) sugar
a pinch of cinnamon
1 egg, beaten
2 teaspoons rose water
250 ml (8 fl oz) single cream

Preheat the oven to 190°C/375°F/Gas Mark 5. Grease a round, glass baking dish, and crumble the pastry into the dish. Mix in the nuts and lemon juice.

Heat the milk, sugar and cinnamon to just below boiling point, then slowly add the beaten egg. Pour this over the pastry mixture in the dish, and sprinkle with rose water. Top with the cream and bake for about 30 minutes, until golden.

*Umm Ali is a very
rich dessert made from
puff pastry, nuts and cream.*

Muhallabia *Ground Rice Pudding*

Serves 6:
1–2 litres (2 pints) milk
2 tablespoons ground rice
1 tablespoon cornflour
5 tablespoons sugar
1 tablespoon rose water
65 g (2 1/2 oz) ground almonds
chopped almonds (or
*   pistachio nuts) to garnish*
grated nutmeg, to sprinkle

With a little of the milk, mix the ground rice and cornflour to a smooth paste.

Slowly heat the sugar in the rest of the milk, and add the rice paste, stirring continuously with a wooden spoon. Simmer the mixture until just below boiling point, and take care not to let it burn on the bottom as this will spoil the delicate flavour. The mixture should thicken in about 15 minutes.

Add the rose water and ground almonds and continue stirring in one direction on a low heat. Simmer for a further 5 minutes, then remove from the heat and cool slightly before pouring the mixture into an attractive glass bowl, or individual glass dishes.

Garnish with almonds or pistachio nuts, and sprinkle with the nutmeg. Leave to chill for about 3-4 hours before serving.

Made from ground rice,
muhallabia is the most
common dessert in the Middle
East. Rose water gives it an
Oriental touch.

Banana Loaf

100 g (4 oz) butter
3 1/2 tablespoons sugar
2 eggs
pinch of cinnamon
1 teaspoon vanilla extract
3 medium ripe bananas
25 g (1 oz) walnuts, coarsely
   chopped
150 g (5 oz) plain flour
2 teaspoons baking powder
1 teaspoon bicarbonate of soda
pinch of salt
1 tablespoon milk

Cream the butter and sugar together, then add the eggs, one at a time, beating after each addition. Add the cinnamon and vanilla and beat well.

Mash the bananas to a pulp, then stir into the mixture together with the walnuts. Combine well, then fold in the sifted dry ingredients alternating with the milk.

Preheat the oven to 180°C/350°F/Gas Mark 5. Line a 23 cm (9 inch) loaf tin with greased greaseproof paper and pour in the mixture. Bake for 50–60 minutes until a skewer comes out clean.

Simple, almost Western, banana loaf from Palestine. Cook with or without walnuts, slice and spread with butter according to taste.

Date Rolls

Makes about 24 rolls:

120 g (4 1/2 oz) plain flour
200 g (7 1/2 oz) unsalted butter, softened
1 tablespoon icing sugar
1 tablespoon oil
1 1/2 tablespoons milk

Filling

1 1/2 tablespoons butter
1 1/2 tablespoons water
350 g (12 oz) dates, stoned and chopped

Make the filling first. Melt the butter together with the water in a saucepan, then add the chopped dates. Cook on a low heat, stirring the dates and pressing down until they become a soft paste. Remove and cool.

To make the dough, sift the flour into a mixing bowl. Cut the soft butter into small pieces and work it into the flour with your fingers. Add the sugar and mix in thoroughly. Make a well in the centre, pour in the oil and milk, then continue to knead the dough until pieces flake off the sides of the bowl. Knead a further 10 minutes, then roll into a ball and chill.

Preheat the oven to 180°C/350°F/Gas Mark 4. Grease a large baking tray. Remove the dough from the refrigerator and divide into

three portions. Knead each well.

On a floured board roll out and flatten a ball of dough. Cut into a neat rectangle shape. Spread one-third of the date mixture thinly over the top. Roll the rectangle into a sausage-shape and continue to roll backwards and forwards until it grows longer and thinner. Slice this into flattened rounds about 4 cm (1 1/2 inch) thick. Repeat this process using the remaining balls of dough.

Place all the slices side by side on the greased baking sheet and prick the tops lightly with a fork. Bake for 25-30 minutes until slightly coloured (if you overcook them, they become hard). Allow to cool, then dust with icing sugar.

Baklava

450 g (1 lb) filo pastry (about
   20 sheets)
100 g (4 oz) unsalted butter,
   melted
100 g (4 oz) chopped pistachio
   nuts or walnuts
1 teaspoon ground cinnamon
1 1/2 tablespoons sugar

Syrup
300 g (11 oz) sugar
75 g (3 oz) honey
450 ml (3/4 pint) water
1 tablespoon lemon juice
1 tablespoon orange flower
   water

Make the syrup first to give it time to chill.
Dissolve all the ingredients together over a
medium heat. Remove from the stove
when the mixture thickens enough to coat
a spoon, cool, then chill thoroughly. Heat the
oven to 180°C/350°F/Gas Mark 4.

Grease a rectangular ovenproof dish
30x20 cm (12x8 inches). Lay 9 of the sheets of
filo in the dish, brushing the top of each with
melted butter as it is laid down.

Mix the nuts, cinnamon and sugar and
spread half over the top filo sheet. Place 2
more buttered sheets on top, and cover with
the rest of the nuts. Layer up the remaining
filo sheets, brushing each with butter as
before. With a sharp knife, cut a diamond
pattern in the top. Sprinkle with water to
prevent the top layers of pastry from curling.

Bake for 30 minutes then increase the oven
temperature to 220°C/425°F/Gas Mark 7.
Bake for a further 10–15 minutes, until the
pastry is puffy and the top is gold. If the top
layer cooks too quickly, cover it with foil, but
do ensure that the pastry is cooked right
through.

Take the *baklava* from the oven and pour
the very cold syrup over the hot pastry.
Leave to cool. When it is cold, cut into
small diamonds and serve.

Above right   *The king of
sweetmeats, baklava has
Turkish origins.*

Right   *Basbousa is one of
many Middle Eastern
sweetmeats made from farina.
Ideal to serve at afternoon tea.*

Basbousa with Coconut

Syrup
100 g (4 oz) sugar
lump of jaggery (if available)
1 tablespoon lemon juice
14 tablespoons
*   boiling water*

Mixture
100 g (4 oz) butter
150 g (5 oz) farina
175 g (6 oz) sugar
50 g (2 oz) shredded coconut
50 g (2 oz) plain flour
50 g (2 oz) milk
1 teaspoon baking powder
few drops of vanilla extract
12 blanched almonds

First make the syrup by dissolving the sugar (and jaggery, if used) in lemon juice and boiling water. Simmer until it thickens, then allow to cool. Preheat oven to 190°C/375°F/Gas Mark 5.

To make the "cake" melt the butter, then pour into a large mixing bowl. Mix in all the other ingredients, and stir well with a wooden spoon. Spoon this mixture into a shallow, Swiss roll tin and flatten the top well.

Bake for about 30 minutes, or until it turns golden. Remove and cut into diamond shapes, placing half an almond on each piece. Pour over half the syrup and bake for a further 5 minutes or until golden brown (do not burn the almonds). Serve warm with the rest of the syrup.

Basbousa are usually eaten hot, but they are also delicious eaten cold. They will keep fresh for several days.

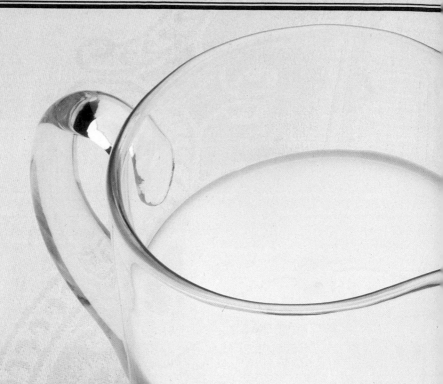

Ramadan Dessert

Serves 10:
450 g (1 lb) dried apricots
225 g (8 oz) dried prunes
100 g (4 oz) mixed dried fruits
*   with peel (raisins, currants,*
*   candied orange peel)*
175 g (6 oz) raisins
4 chopped dried figs
*   (optional)*
600 ml (1 pint) water
50 g (2 oz) sugar
100 g (4 oz) mixed nuts (pine
*   nuts, walnuts,*
*   almonds), chopped*
single cream, to serve
grated nutmeg, to decorate

Soak all the fruit overnight. Bring the water and sugar to the boil in a large saucepan. Stir 15-20 minutes, or until it becomes a syrupy consistency. Add all the fruits and simmer 1½–2 hours. After 1 hour add the nuts and mix well.

Remove the mixture from the heat and allow to cool then chill. Serve in a cut glass bowl or individual dishes. Pour single cream over the top and garnish with grated nutmeg.

Ramadan dessert is eaten when the Muslim fast is over at dusk.

Stuffed Dates

450 g (1 lb) fresh dates, stoned
Almond Paste
100 g (4 oz) blanched almonds
1 large egg white
175 g (6 oz) icing sugar
2 teaspoons almond extract
2 drops rose water
green food colouring, as desired

Preheat the oven to 160°C/325°F/Gas Mark 3. Spread the almonds on a baking sheet and bake for 10 minutes, or until they are oily, but not brown. Cool, then grind in a food processor.

Add the egg white, sugar and almond extract, and process to give a firm paste. Add rose water, food colouring if using, and blend briefly. Chill overnight.

Open each date along the side it has been stoned and press a small amount of paste into each.

Stuffed dates are made on special occasions such as the Eid al-fitr holiday.

Almond Fingers

Makes about 30 fingers:
12 sheets filo pastry
100 g (4 oz) unsalted butter,
  melted
50 g (2 oz) sugar
100 g (4 oz) ground almonds
pinch of ground cinnamon
1 teaspoon rose water
icing sugar, to sprinkle

Slice each filo sheet into three rectangles. Brush each rectangle with the melted butter. Preheat the oven to 160°C/325°F/Gas Mark 3.

Mix the sugar, almonds, cinnamon and rose water together, and place about a teaspoon of this in the centre of each rectangle. Fold the sides in and roll into a cigar shape.

Place in rows on a greased baking sheet and cook for 30 minutes, or until the pastry turns pale gold. Remove, cool and dust with icing sugar.

Almond fingers are dainty sweetmeats dating from medieval times.

Orange Slices with Cinnamon

Serves 4:

Choose navel oranges if possible. Peel and
slice 3 oranges thinly, removing any pith
and seeds. Arrange on a glass dish and
sprinkle with ground cinnamon. Chill,
then remove from the refrigerator 10
minutes before serving.

Figs with Orange Juice

Serves 4:

This is a simple dessert which can be
prepared in advance. Cut the stalks off
about twelve fresh figs, but do not peel
them. Quarter them and arrange in a
flower effect on a dish. Cover with orange
juice and chill.

Date and Banana Dessert

Serves 4:

*450 g (1 lb) fresh dates, stoned
    and halved.*
4 bananas
250 ml (8 fl oz) single cream
*25 g (1 oz) roughly chopped
    walnuts*
freshly grated nutmeg

Fill either a glass bowl or individual glass
dishes with alternate layers of halved dates
and bananas. The dates should be as fresh as
possible and should not be soft.

Cover with cream and chill for at least 2
hours so the dates will absorb the cream.

Garnish with walnuts and freshly grated
nutmeg and serve.

*Easy to prepare chilled
desserts: figs with orange juice
(above left), cinnamon
orange slices (above right),
and date and banana
(below).*

Next page   *A selection of
typically Middle Eastern
fruits.*

Beverages

lcohol is forbidden by the
Quran. This is not to say that
several countries do not produce
some palatable wines: Turkey,
Syria and Lebanon are wine
producers and to a lesser extent,
Egypt. The fiery aperitif *arak* is
drunk in the Levant. The Turks
drink it throughout the *mezze,* in
fact a *mezze* without *arak* (or *rakı*) is
unthinkable.

Muslim families commonly
drink mineral water or soft drinks
with their meals. Lebanon bottles
mineral water, and the tiny Gulf
emirate of Ajman supplies the
whole of Arabia with fine mineral
water from an inland spring.

The ringing of the water seller's
bell is still a familiar sound
throughout the Middle East and in
Egypt in particular. The bearer of
news, the water seller has an
important rank in street society. In
the old days other street vendors
used to sell fruit juices from glass
flasks strapped onto their backs;
today rows of juicers whizz in
sidewalk cafés. Only in poor rural
communities will you find
someone still squeezing oranges, or
pressing sugar cane on a crude
machine salvaged from
automobile parts.

Fresh lemon, or better still fresh
lime juice, is my favourite cool drink
on a hot day. In 1964, after travelling
across North Africa, I spent some
time staying with my cousin who
worked at the British Embassy in
Cairo. Each afternoon, an old lime
seller used to call at her flat in
Zamalek and on hearing his call from
the street below, she would lower a
basket for limes for our gin and
tonics. And I particularly remember a

tangy *limoonada* which revived me
after a morning spent photographing
the ruins of Persepolis, in Iran.

The ancient Persians were
masters at making effervescent
sharbats or sherbets from oranges,
limes, apricots and other fruits. The
pomegranate is a favourite fruit in
Iran – it is said that the Prophet
Muhammed urged his followers to
eat it because it purged the system
of envy and hatred. Using vivid
metaphors, poets from Ferdowsi to
the present day have compared the
pomegranate to a woman's womb,
ripe with progeny, to young
maiden's cheeks and the opened
fruit to a broken heart, the seeds
like tears of blood.

Tamarind juice is another
popular beverage, especially in
Syria and Iraq. The drink of
nomads, yoghurt and water, is
commonly drunk with meals in
Turkey and Yemen. Crushed
almonds and milk is the stuff of the
Arabian Nights.

Tea spiced with ginger and
cinnamon is popular, but coffee,
and the making and serving of
coffee, has pride of place in Middle
Eastern folklore, the whole coffee
ritual being like a silent language
that binds both host and guest.

In traditional Bedouin society, a
guest is invited to take his place
around the fire in the men's section
of the tent. The host then digs into
the coffee-bag and puts some beans
in a ladle to roast on the embers.
When they have cooled, he pounds
them with a pestle and mortar or
mihbash of traditional carved wood,
or brass.

A skilful coffee grinder can
pound out an appreciable rhythm

*The Middle Eastern coffee
ceremony is like a silent
language binding both host
and guest. Twigs act as a filter
in the spout. Photographed in
Wadi Rum, Jordan.*

audible at some distance, announcing to neighbours the arrival of a guest. The beans are tossed into boiling water and after boiling several times, the contents are poured into another pot and a pinch of freshly ground cardamom is added. This is allowed to simmer for about 15 minutes, the pleasant aroma pervading the whole tent.

The following gestures, now largely symbolic, remain essential protocol in the basic Bedouin coffee ceremony of the Middle East.

The first cup, offered to the host, is deemed the "unworthy cup"; assuring the guest that the coffee is safe to drink and confirming to the host that it is hot, since it is a terrible insult to serve cold coffee. Like the other cups, the second cup is poured with the left hand, the bearer palming the tiny white china cups in his right. This cup is offered to the guest whose acceptance signifies that he is pleased with the hospitality.

The third cup, even more significantly, has its roots in the days of tribal feuds. It silently concludes the protection agreement, meaning that the guest is safe from any attack while under the auspices of his host. This cup, known as the "sword cup", is binding, even against attack by one or the other's relatives. Sometimes a fourth cup is offered, confirming the silent defence pact.

It is not usual to drink more than this, but if a guest wants more (only a few drops are poured into each cup) he simply holds out his cup to be refilled by the attentive bearer. Alternatively, to signify he has had enough, he flicks the cup a couple of times with his wrist, the final concluding gesture to the coffee ritual.

Unfortunately, "Turkish coffee" as it is known in the West, is growing rare. High prices on the world coffee bean market have put many Middle Eastern coffee houses out of business and in Mocha, the famous coffee port in North Yemen, there is not even a drop of Nescafé! Chasing the quick profits from *qat*, local farmers have torn out their traditional coffee bushes and instead planted *Catha edulis (qat)*.

Qahwa (Arabic for coffee) uses coffee grounds and cardamom pods in varying quantities. It is served at every opportunity. You can be seated only seconds in someone's home or office when, like a genie (or *djinn* in Arabic), a bearer arrives with a pot of *qahwa* and a stack of tiny cups.

I especially recall an early morning in Dubai when I drove into the desert to watch Bedouin training a young falcon. Seated in their tent, I was invited to share their humble breakfast of bread, sandy dates and *qahwa*. No race is more hospitable than the Bedouin who will go without rather than have nothing to offer.

Yoghurt Drink

Serves 8:
900 ml (1 ½ pints) natural yoghurt
1.25 litres (2 ¼ pints) iced water
1 tablespoon finely
  chopped fresh mint
pinch of salt

Mix all the ingredients together and pour into glasses, garnishing each with a little extra mint. Using sparkling mineral water rather than iced water makes an even more refreshing drink. Serve well chilled.

Yoghurt drink (above left) is especially popular in Iran and Turkey. Almond drink (above right) echoes the Arabian Nights.

Almond Drink

Serves 6:
165 g (5 ½ oz) blanched almonds
sugar, to taste
350 ml (12 fl oz) water
600 ml (1 pint) milk
1 teaspoon orange blossom
  water
few drops of almond extract

Chop the almonds and combine in a blender with the sugar and water. Blend until smooth, then add the remaining ingredients. Garnish each glass with a rose petal.

Middle Eastern Lemonade

Serves 6:
8 lemons
150 g (5 oz) sugar, or to taste
1 teaspoon orange blossom water,
    or to taste
generous 2 tablespoons
    freshly chopped mint
still or sparkling water
ice cubes

Squeeze the juice from the lemons and
sweeten to taste with the sugar. Add the
orange blossom water and the mint, and
stir or shake well together. Pour a little into
a tall glass and fill with water and ice.

*Popular thirst quenchers
throughout the Middle East
are lemon, orange and colourful
pomegranate juice.*

Orange Sharbat

Serves 6:
16 medium oranges
sugar, to taste
1 teaspoon orange blossom
    water
water and ice cubes
sprigs of fresh mint, to garnish

Squeeze the juice from the oranges and
sweeten to taste with the sugar. Add the
orange blossom water and mix well. Serve
diluted with ice cold water and garnished
with mint.

Pomegranate Drink

Serves 4-6:
600 ml (1 pint) pomegranate juice
120 ml (4 fl oz) lemon juice
1 teaspoon orange blossom
    water
sugar, to taste
sparkling or still mineral
    water

Combine everything in a blender, or mix
well in a pitcher and serve with ice cubes.

Turkish Coffee

There are three ways of ordering coffee in Arabic, and these are: sweet (*helou* or *sukkar ziada*), medium (*mazbout*) or unsweetened (*murra*). Sugar is boiled with the coffee and the quantity will depend on the preference of your guests. This recipe is for medium coffee, to give an idea of the sugar quantities. If other guests require *helou* coffee, or no sugar at all, then you must brew another pot. Even if you like ordinary coffee without sugar, it is rare to drink Turkish coffee, as it is so sharp, without some sweetening.

Serves 2:
3 tablespoons roasted ground coffee
1 heaped teaspoon sugar
2 small coffee cups water
tiny pinch of ground cardamom

Combine all the ingredients in a long handled coffee pot or tiny saucepan, stir well and bring to the boil. As the froth forms on top, remove from the stove, stir again and return to the heat until the froth rises again. Be very careful it does not boil over. Boil it briefly again, then stand aside for a few seconds.

Have the small cups ready to pour in the coffee, raising the pot (difficult with a saucepan) to get a nice head of froth on each cup. The grounds should be allowed to settle a minute or two before the coffee is drunk.

Rose Petal Tea

Serves 4:
handful rose petals
600 ml (1 pint) water
honey, to taste

Choose fresh rose petals. Strip the flower gently under running water then place the petals in a saucepan. Cover with the water and boil for 5 minutes, or until the petals become discoloured. Strain into teacups and add honey to taste.

Qahwa *Arab Coffee*

Serves 6:
6 cardamom pods
175 ml (6 fl oz) cold water
1 heaped tablespoon dark roast coffee, coarsely ground

Turkish coffee (left), rose petal tea (centre) and qahwa (right). Turkish coffee is dark and strong. Qahwa is rather bitter. All are common hot beverages throughout the Middle East.

Bruise the cardamom pods by pounding gently in a pestle and mortar. Using a long handled coffee pot (or a tiny saucepan), place in it the water, pods and coffee. Bring to the boil, then simmer on a low heat for 15 minutes until the grounds settle.

Serve *qahwa* in tiny white coffee cups – Arabic ones do not have handles – about 2 tablespoons in each. *Qahwa* is not served with sugar, and its rather bitter flavour is not to everyone's taste. It is traditional Arabic coffee.

Index

Almond drink 145
Almond fingers 137
Arabian cuisine 13–14
Arab chopped salad 57
Arab coffee 149
Artichoke hearts in olive oil 31
Asparagus salad 62
Aubergine:
    Baked 67
    Baked with cumin 68
    Dip 23
    Salad 58

Babagannouj – aubergine dip 23
Baked aubergines 67
Baked courgettes in tahini sauce 73
Baked fish with saffron rice 118
Baked squash with cumin 68
Baklava 132
Banana and date dessert 140
Banana loaf 130
Barbecued fish with dates 119
Basbousa with coconut 133
Batata charp – stuffed potatoes 66
Bean stew 70
Beid bi limoun – egg and lemon
    soup 44
Beid ghanam – lambs' testicles 36
Brains in lemon and olive oil 36
Bread 6–7
Butter bean rissoles 28

Cabbage rolls 69
"Caliph's delight" 126
Carrot soup 46
Casseroles:
    Chick pea and lamb 87
    Lemon chicken 98
    Okra and lamb 86
    Persian with prunes 81
    String bean 70
    Turkish vegetable 74
Chelo – Persian steamed rice 76
Chick pea dip 24
Chick pea and lamb casserole 87
Chicken:
    Circassian chicken 104
    Grilled lemon chicken 108
    Hot chicken 100
    Kebabs 107
    Lemon chicken casserole 98
    Musakhan chicken 102
    Olives with chicken 109
    Persian chicken 103
    Roast, stuffed with rice and nuts 106
    Wings with garlic and yoghurt 38
    Yoghurt and chicken 99
Chilled cucumber and yoghurt soup 46

Coconut with basbousa 133
Coffee:
    Turkish 149
    Arab 149
Cold fish in olive oil 113
Courgette soup 51
Courgettes with tomatoes 70
Cucumber and raisin salad with
    yoghurt 58
Curry (prawn) 114

Dates:
    Date and banana dessert 138
    Dates with barbecued fish 119
    Date Ma'amoul – date rolls 131
    Date rolls 131
    Stuffed dates 136
Dietary laws 17
Dolma – stuffed vine leaves 26
Dried fruit salad 134
Duck in walnut and pomegranate
    sauce 110

Egg and lemon soup 44
Egyptian cuisine 13
Etiquette 17

Falafel – chick pea rissoles 28
Fattouche – mixed vegetable and
    bread salad 56
Feast-day soup 48
Ferakh al-hara – hot chicken 100
Festivals 20
Figs with orange juice 138
Fish:
    Baked with saffron rice 118
    Baked in tahini sauce 121
    Barbecued with dates 119
    Cold in olive oil 113
    Fried 116
    In hot sauce 120
    Roe dip 24
    Soup 45
French bean stew 70
French bean, leek and
    asparagus salad 62
Fruit salad (dried) 134

Green pepper salad 60

Herb and nut omelette 72
Hot pepper dip – muhammara 28
Hummus – chick pea dip 24

Imam bayıldı 67
Iraqi cuisine 16–17

Jordanian cuisine 8, 11

Kadın Budu – "Lady's thighs" 34
Kebabs:
    Chicken 107
    Minced meat 92
    Turkish style 93
Kibbeh bi laban – meat balls 89
Kibbeh nayé – raw seasoned meat with
    bulghur 35
Khoubz Arabieh – Arab bread 41
Kidney bean salad 55
Kidneys in tomato sauce 95

Labneh – thick yoghurt 27
"Lady's thighs" – kadın budu 34
Lamb:
    Braised chops and vegetables 88
    and chick pea casserole 87
    and okra stew 86
    Roast leg with yoghurt and lemon 85
    Roast stuffed neck 82
    Shoulder with saffron 84
Lebanese cuisine 8, 10
Lebanese "National" salad 30
Leek salad 62
Lemonade 146
Lentil soup 48
Liver (fried) 36

Meatballs 89
Meatloaf (Syrian) 94
Middle Eastern lemonade 146
Muhallabia – ground rice pudding 129
Muhammara – hot pepper dip 28
Mussels (fried) 38

North Yemen 6
Nut and herb omelette 72

Okra and lamb stew 86
Okra stew 71
Orange juice with figs 140
Orange sharbat 146
Orange slices with cinnamon 138

Pepper dip (hot) 28
Persian casserole with prunes 81
Persian cuisine 15–16
Pickled chilli peppers 40
Plain pilaf rice 76
Pomegranate drink 147
Potato salad 60
Potatoes (stuffed) 66
Prawns in tomato sauce 117

Qahwa – Arab coffee 149

Raisin and cucumber salad with yoghurt 58
Ramadan dessert – dried fruit salad 134

Rice:
    Ground rice pudding 129
    Persian steamed rice – chelo 76
    Plain pilaf rice 76
    Saffron rice 76
Roast stuffed neck of lamb 82
Rose petal tea 149

Saffron rice 76
Salata Arabieh – Arab chopped salad 57
Salata fil-fil – sweet green pepper salad 60
Samak al-hara – fish in hot sauce 120
Sanbusak – stuffed crescent
    pastries 32, 33
Saudi Arabian cuisine 6
Sesame paste dip – tahini 24
Shoulder of lamb with saffron 84
Spices 17-18
Spinach pie 75
Spinach salad 58
Squash baked in tahini sauce 73
Squid – stuffed 123
Stuffed:
    Crescent pastries 32, 33
    Potatoes 66
    Tomatoes 66
    Vine leaves 26
Syrian cuisine 8, 10-11
Syrian meatloaf 94
Syrian stuffed kibbeh 90

Tabbouleh – Lebanese "National"
    salad 30
Tahini – sesame paste dip 24
Tahini sauce with baked fish 121
Tahini sauce with baked squash 73
Taramasalata – fish roe dip 24
Thick yoghurt 27
Tomato:
    and coriander salad 60
    sauce with kidneys 95
    sauce with prawns 117
    soup 52
    Stuffed 66
Tuna shashlik 122
Turkish coffee 149
Turkish cuisine 11-13
Turkish style kebabs 93
Turkish vegetable casserole 74

Umm Ali – "Mother of Ali" 127

Vegetable and bread salad 56
Vegetable casserole 74
Vegetable soup 50
Vine leaves (stuffed) 26

Yemeni cuisine 14–15

Yoghurt:
    with chicken 99
    Drink 145
    Thick 27
    Soup 46

Spice Names

The following are Arabic translations of the most commonly used spices – a handy guide for shopping in the *souqs*:

Allspice: *bahar*
Anise: *anisun*
Black Pepper: *fil-fil afwad*
Cardamom: *hayl (habahan)*
Chilli: *fil-fil ahmar har*
Cloves: *kabsh qaranful*
Coriander: *kusbarah*
Cumin: *kammun*
Fenugreek: *helba*
Ginger: *zanjibil*
Mace: *fuljan*
Nutmeg: *jawz al-teeb*
Paprika: *fil-fil ahmar*
Saffron: *za'fran*
Sesame seed: *sim-sim*
Tamarind: *tammar al-Hindi*
Tumeric: *kurkum*

Acknowledgements

I would like to thank Gulf Air, the national carrier of Bahrain, Qatar, the United Arab Emirates and the Sultanate of Oman for helping with this project. Gulf Air is the only Middle Eastern airline member of the Chaine des Rôtisseurs: Gulf seafood, dates and Arab coffee are local delicacies on their menu. I would also like to thank the Bahrain and Kuwait Hiltons for their hospitality. All the Middle East Hiltons are renowned for excellent food, ethnic buffets being a special feature. The Sheraton Hotel in Sana'a was most helpful during difficult research in North Yemen. In London, Barbara Tobias, Aileen Aitken, Joan Parker, Raghad Ahmed, Abdul Latif Salazar, Akın Urs and other friends were especially encouraging. Special thanks, go to my editor, Susan Fleming, home economist Norman Miller, and to Multimedia's Chief Editor, Anne Cope. Part of the introduction to the Beverages section is reproduced from my book *An Insight and Guide to Jordan* published by Longman (1981).

CHRISTINE OSBORNE

PICTURE CREDITS

Theo Bergström   12, 20–1, 24–5, 26–7, 28–9, 30–1, 32–3, 34–5, 36–7, 38–9, 40–1, 45, 46–7, 48–9, 50–1, 52, 55, 56–7, 58–9, 60–1, 62–3, 66–7, 70–1, 72–3, 74–5, 76–7, 82–3, 85, 86, 88–9, 90–1, 92, 94–5, 98, 100–1, 102–3, 104–5, 106, 108–9, 110, 113, 114–5, 116, 119, 120–1, 126–7, 128–9, 130, 132–3 top, 134–5, 137, 138–9, 140–1, 144–5, 146–7, 148–9, front and back endpapers

Michael Boys Syndication   15

Christine Osborne   title page, contents page, 7, 9, 10, 16, 19, 42–3, 53, 65, 78–9 centre and right, 96–7, 111, 124–5, 143

Paris Graphic   front and back jacket and cover, 23, 44, 68–9, 81, 84, 87, 93, 99, 107, 117, 118, 122, 123, 131, 132–3 bottom, 136

Multimedia Publications (UK) Ltd have endeavoured to observe the legal requirements with respect to suppliers of photographic material.